CORPORATE

CULTURE

DEMYSTIFIED

First edition published in March 2020

Paperback ISBN: 978-1-77934-168-6
Publisher: Marc Pillay – Demystifying Life
Email: lifedemystified.inc@gmail.com
Author page: https://www.amazon.com/author/marcpillay

Editing: Wesley Thompson
Cover: wim@wimrheeder.co.za
Text design: Book Lingo

bⱮk
lingo

publish@booklingo.co.za

Set in 11 point on 15 point, Caecilia LT Std
Printed and bound by Digital Action, Cape Town

CORPORATE CULTURE
DEMYSTIFIED

WHY GOOD BUSINESS STRATEGIES FAIL

MARC PILLAY

MARC PILLAY

DEMYSTIFYING LIFE

amazon

Amazon Author Page

https://www.amazon.com/author/marcpillay

https://www.facebook.com/
marcpillay.demystifyinglife/

@MarcPillay3

@pillay_marc

ABOUT THE AUTHOR

Marc Pillay is a lawyer by profession, and a member of the Law Society of Zimbabwe.

He has more than 15 years of diversified experience in legal practice and as corporate legal counsel, human resources manager, compliance manager and non-executive director across various business sectors, including energy, retail, mining, financial services and pharmaceuticals.

Marc is also a writer and a life-analyst. He aims to demystify a host of life situations by candidly questioning conventional wisdom and the status quo; by analysing common life scenarios and continuously aiming to unpack them in a way that provides practical, day-to-day value; by asking real questions applicable to real-life situations; and by giving real answers that real people can identify with and apply to improve their lives.

This is Marc's second published book in the *Demystified* series, succeeding *Life Demystified* (first and second editions). Several of his articles have been published in the national press in Zimbabwe.

This book is the second in the *Demystified* series, following *Life Demystified*, which is referenced several times.

By purchasing this book – *Corporate Culture Demystified* (paperback or ebook) – you qualify to receive a FREE PDF version of *Life Demystified* IMMEDIATELY, as well as selected free chapters of forthcoming publications on an ongoing basis.

Simply email:
lifedemystified.inc@gmail.com.

CONTENTS

PREFACE

GIVE YOURSELF THE REAL COMPETITIVE ADVANTAGE

"Corporate culture is the only sustainable competitive advantage that is completely within the control of the entrepreneur. Develop a strong corporate culture first and foremost."

This powerful and profound quote from David Cummings, co-founder of Pardot, provides the perfect starting point as I embark on this quest to demystify corporate culture* and illustrate just how important it is, and how it feeds into every facet of an organisation.

We've all seen the same things at play, almost on a daily basis. Internal politics; bureaucracies; adhocracies; silos; excessive (and unproductive) meetings; tasks not being completed in line with undertakings; processes and procedures not being followed; and finger-pointing and the blame game.

The terms "corporate culture" and "organisational culture" are used interchangeably throughout this book.

I could go on and on. And I'm sure we've all been part of it to some extent – whether dishing it out, being on the receiving end of it or, most likely, both.

From small, family-run businesses to the largest of corporations, the same flaws and deficiencies can be seen routinely manifesting themselves. And many a CEO will often sit quietly (and probably despondently) pondering and contemplating why, oh why, these things keep happening.

These continuing flaws and deficiencies inevitably have a negative impact on business strategies – on *good* business strategies – that have been painstakingly devised. Business strategies whose implementation every CEO is accountable to the board and shareholders for. The common result is executive management meetings being held and action plans formulated to eradicate these deficiencies. These will often include measures such as restructuring; changing job descriptions; and amending policies, procedures and processes or introducing new ones. These action plans are diligently implemented yet, still, the problems persist.

A common conclusion arrived at by executive management is that there is a human-capital gap. In other words, the people we have are simply not capable of doing what we expect them to do. And, to take it a step further, this is often the position that is formally communicated to the board and shareholders.

This, in my opinion, is a lazy conclusion and an

easy way out. It is a conclusion that allows business leaders to exonerate themselves of any blame relating to these continuing deficiencies within the business. These continuing deficiencies within the business which they, as business leaders, have failed to eradicate.

I am firmly of the view, however, that all flaws, deficiencies and overall inefficiencies within a business can and should be traced back to the leadership as the people who set the corporate culture and have not only the power, but also the duty to reshape and change it when necessary. My view, in a nutshell, which is unpacked in a number of different contexts in each chapter, is quite simply:

Everything that happens and doesn't happen in a business is a symptom of the corporate or organisational culture. Everything!

PART I
INTRODUCTION TO
CORPORATE CULTURE

CHAPTER I

WHAT IS ORGANISATIONAL CULTURE?

It was early 2019. I was driving along the streets of my beloved Harare, Zimbabwe, primarily focused on navigating my way around the potholes, which have now become the accepted norm. I got a pleasant surprise as I approached a set of traffic lights that was actually working, but my mood quickly changed when, as had become the norm, someone pulled up beside me, trying to perform an illegal manoeuvre. I lowered my window and angrily asked him, "What are you trying to do?" quickly following up with an incensed directive to "go and learn the rules of the road!" with one or two vulgarities thrown in for good measure. I was initially quite taken aback by what followed.

"There are no rules in Zimbabwe!" was his simple, matter-of-fact retort.

But as my anger subsided and I continued on my journey, I began to think more about this response I had been given, but from a less emotional perspective. And I found it to be quite insightful and thought-provoking. This experience, and especially the retort from this law-breaking motorist, opened up my eyes to an entirely different dimension of laws, rules and indeed culture.

It is a fact that there are rules and laws that exist in Zimbabwe. I knew this, and the other driver knew this. But despite the known existence of these rules and laws, this motorist's response was a very clear indication of the way things have, most unfortunately, evolved and, dare I say decayed in Zimbabwe. In many aspects of life, there is total disregard for whatever rules and laws there are in existence, and that has become the norm. Despite what governmental, parliamentary and judicial officers may say about rules and laws, the common man on the street says that there are no rules in Zimbabwe! It has, quite simply, become the culture of Zimbabwean society. And visitors to this country will, almost certainly, return home with the view that Zimbabwe is a lawless society.

In the corporate context, Scott Berkun summed it up perfectly when he said, "Every CEO is in fact a Chief Cultural Officer. The terrifying thing is it's the CEO's actual behavior, not their speeches or the list of values they have put up on posters, that defines what the culture is."

Professionalism; innovation; empowerment; compliance; transparency; and accountability. These are among the most common answers that will be routinely rattled off by business leaders when faced with the question, "What is the organisational culture here?"

But the more important question is – or at least ought to be – whether the people in an organisation, other than its leaders, would give the same answers. Because here's the thing … The culture of an organisation, or society for that matter, is *not* what the leaders of that organisation or society say it is. Rather, it is what the ordinary person within that organisation or society says it is; and what people from the outside looking in say it is.

In line with the above, it is my view that organisational culture has two major elements. The first is the culture within, which dictates and directs the way the people within an organisation deal with each other. From the leaders (the CEO and executive management) to middle management, down to the lowest-graded employee. They all deal with each other on a daily basis in a certain manner that, whether good or bad, has become acceptable. The second is the way these same people deal with external parties.

These two are distinct from, yet influence each other. The culture within, that is, the accepted way in which the people in an organisation deal with each other, will inevitably have a major influence on the way the same people behave in their dealings with external parties. Let's look at a couple of simple but common examples. If everyone within the organisation greets each other by saying "Hi" rather than "Good morning", then it is most probable that they will do the same with external parties. And if everyone within the organisation – from the CEO down – addresses each other by their first name, then it is most probable that external parties will also be addressed by their first name rather than as "Mr So-and-so". And for this reason, the "culture within" – as I call it – will be the focus of this chapter and the book as a whole.

I have worked for a number of organisations in the commercial sector, ranging from family-owned businesses to corporates, for close to 15 years. And before moving into the commercial sector, I had the benefit of working as an attorney in private practice for over four years, during which period I necessarily had significant dealings with a large number of corporate clients, which inevitably revealed much about the organisational culture within those corporates. It is from these experiences that I have come up with certain insights into and views on organisational culture.

While organisational culture is undoubtedly a partial product of what the organisation formally documents – including the creation of a vision; a mission; values; strategies; and policies – it is not exclusively so. Far from it! In far too many cases, the mission, values and policies that are in place represent only a theoretical state of affairs which is far removed from reality. They represent what is likely to be favourably interpreted by stakeholders looking from the outside in.

Organisational culture, to a far greater extent,

is a product of the *unwritten* rules. The rules that, somewhat miraculously, are very well known to everybody within the organisation without anyone ever having formally communicated them. The rules that everyone in the organisation obeys and abides by, religiously, despite the fact that they may actually be, and often are, contrary to what is documented in the said vision, mission, values, strategies and policies. Every organisation, no matter how big or small, has these unwritten yet non-negotiable rules. These are the culture-defining rules. I'm pretty certain that every person who has ever been formally employed has, at some point, either told someone or been told, "We don't do xyz around here …" Again, we'll look at a simple example. Invariably, every organisation will have clearly defined and documented office hours, whether in each person's employment contract or in a Conditions of Service Policy. So, for example, you may find that office hours are 8am to 4.30pm. So, most likely, a new employee will begin packing up at 4.30pm and will be out of the door by 4.35pm. But he will soon realise, if a colleague does not tell him as much, that despite the official 4.30pm close of business, nobody leaves before 5pm. This is the unwritten rule that everyone abides by, and if you don't, you will be frowned upon.

These unwritten rules also include the manner in which strategic issues are treated and communicated (or, more often, *not* communicated); decision-making from top to bottom; and the general perception of, and belief about, various common workplace concepts such as teamwork, customer service, people management, approachability, and openness to new or different ideas. These, and others, are examined and unpacked individually chapter by chapter.

So, to get back to the very beginning – the title of this chapter – what is organisational culture?

Organisational culture is the common set of day-to-day behaviours, beliefs and expectations of all the people within an organisation regardless of what is formally documented.

CHAPTER 2

CULTURAL ENTROPY

"If you can't measure it, you can't manage it, and if you can't manage it, you can't change it."

These are the wise words of Harvard Professor Robert Kaplan. In the context of corporate culture, if you are serious about changing it, you must be able to manage it. And, in line with Professor Kaplan's thought process, you must, therefore, be able to measure the existing corporate culture and keep tracking it as this culture-change journey progresses. The reality of corporate life is that new CEOs are almost routinely appointed with the primary mandate to change the corporate culture. Where does a new CEO in this situation begin?

Culture – whether corporate or otherwise – is one of those things that falls within a somewhat problematic category known as "the intangibles". The things that are difficult (some would say impossible) to quantitatively measure. There is, however, a school of thought which says, quite simply, "If it exists, it can be measured." And I have noticed, particularly in the corporate environment, that there is indeed an underlying compulsion to measure almost everything. I unpack, in detail, what I call "the misguided compulsion to measure" in my previous book, *Life Demystified*. In a nutshell, measuring is inherently good and necessary. But if you're tracking and measuring the wrong things, you are fooling yourself, and you may as well not be measuring anything at all! And this is where cultural entropy comes in.

So, what is cultural entropy? It is actually a term that I had not come across before I set about writing this book. And my educated guess is that many business executives would, similarly, not have come across it before reading this book. Indeed, I have sat through several strategic planning sessions where hours have been spent – ultimately unsuccessfully – discussing, debating and trying to define and measure corporate culture. Yet, in all those hours, never was there as much as a mention of this thing called cultural entropy. I have since come to realise that cultural entropy is a vital component in my quest to demystify corporate culture. A good appreciation, not only of the meaning of this concept, but also of its very existence, is critical to understanding and changing the prevailing organisational culture.

So, to repeat the question: What is cultural entropy? There are a number of helpful definitions

I have come across, which define cultural entropy as:

- "the level of dysfunction in an organization that is created as a result of fear-driven energy";
- "the amount of energy consumed in an organisation on doing unproductive work";
- "a measure of the friction and pent-up frustration that exists within an organization"; and
- "the amount of negative or limiting values that exist within an organisation resulting in unproductive employees".

From these definitions we begin to see that, in a nutshell, cultural entropy is actually a measure of the existing corporate culture. And for any business leader who is serious about culture transformation in their organisation, getting an accurate measure of what/where it is to start with is non-negotiable. This is done, first and foremost, by establishing the existing cultural entropy.

Cultural transformation is a journey. And to successfully plan any journey, you need to know where you're starting from!

Cultural entropy has an inverse relationship with the other aspect of any organisation that gives major insight into the corporate culture: employee engagement (which we look at in more detail in Chapter 17). In a nutshell, the higher the cultural entropy, the lower the employee engagement, as shown in Figure 2.1.

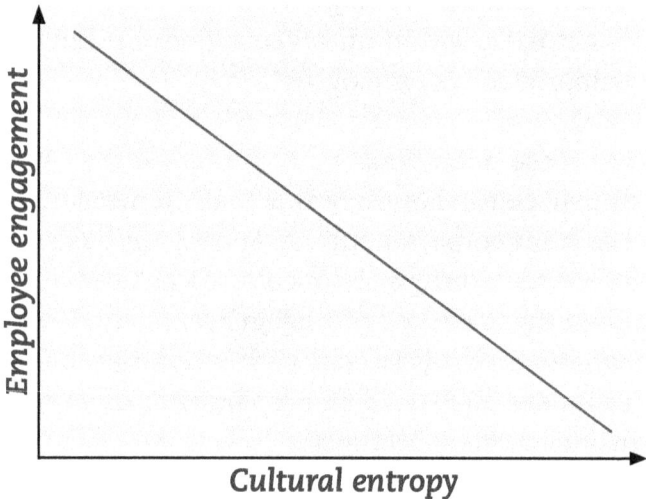

Figure 2.1: The inverse relationship between employee engagement and cultural entropy

The cornerstone of *Life Demystified* is *understanding*, and we look at this more in Chapter 5. I see this as the most critical component in achieving anything. And understanding requires one to ask, and answer with brutal honesty, the question *why*. So, after establishing *what* the cultural entropy is, the next step is to get down to the nitty-gritty of *why* it is as it is. Only then can you hope to change it.

Some of the given definitions begin to answer the *why*. A major reason for high levels of cultural entropy is, in a nutshell, fear. And applying my own experience-based logic, fear in the corporate environment has two major elements. First, is the obvious and understandable fear of losing one's job and with it one's livelihood, if you speak up. The result of this fear is that all the frustration, friction and general negative emotions become pent-up in employees. The second element of fear in the workplace is its source. It can only be the business leaders who have either created the culture of fear or, if they have not created it, have chosen not to address it and thus have perpetuated it. In the law of Delict, or Tort, a person is deemed equally as culpable for his omission as he is for his action. It is neither good enough at law nor in the corporate context to turn a blind eye and say, "But I didn't do it." So, consequently, it can only be business leaders, through deliberate and concerted efforts, who eliminate this fear and, with it, reduce the levels of cultural entropy.

This fear, however, presents a paradox of sorts. The only way to establish the cultural entropy, and indeed the employee-engagement levels in an organisation, is to engage the employees – whether through a survey or through some other method. But if fear is already prevalent, then any survey or other engagement is likely to be a pointless exercise because this pre-existing fear will inhibit the levels of honesty coming out of those engagements.

The purpose of this book, and of this chapter, is not really to provide answers on how cultural entropy, or indeed the very closely linked employee engagement, can be accurately established and how organisational culture can be changed. Those questions are for business leaders to answer for themselves – with or without the help of experts on the subject – starting by taking into account the idiosyncrasies and circumstances relevant to their own respective businesses. The purpose, rather, is to highlight, and demonstrate through real examples that the reader can easily identify with, the importance of organisational culture in day-to-day corporate life, and the critical need to keep measuring it and keep actively transforming it as required.

The purpose of this chapter is, quite simply, to highlight the existence and critical value of this thing called cultural entropy.

Establishing and understanding the pre-vailing cultural entropy are the necessary first steps on the road to culture change.

PART II
STRATEGY AND
CULTURE

CHAPTER 3

CULTURE VERSUS STRATEGY: THE RUNNING BATTLE

"Culture eats strategy for breakfast."

Despite these wise words from management guru, Peter Drucker, little regard is generally given to the corporate culture during the strategy-setting process. Lengthy brainstorming and strategy-planning sessions are held annually, quarterly and even monthly by businesses, big and small. Brilliant ideas are canvassed and then, often painstakingly, transformed into strategic plans to be implemented over the next year or two or five.

Policies, processes and procedures – the rules – are meticulously crafted, reviewed, re-reviewed and eventually approved for implementation in support of achieving the strategic goals that have been painstakingly set. These rules are formally documented and, ideally, communicated to everyone within the business. The rules, which are aimed at achieving certain strategic objectives, are now firmly in place. I'm sure this sounds all too familiar.

Before going any further, it is perhaps worth looking back on the experience I shared in Chapter 1, when a motorist told me, in no uncertain terms, that there are no rules in Zimbabwe. He said this not because he genuinely thought that there were no rules in existence, but because to him, and indeed to large sections of society, the rules that I may have been referring to were merely theoretical and had no impact or implication on the way day-to-day life unfolds in reality. He held this view because a certain culture had developed over time. A culture that says that despite the existence of certain rules, "we can do as we please".

This principle has very similar application in the corporate world and, in particular, in the implementation of business strategies. The rules that have been deliberated upon and set in order to achieve strategic objectives will be seen as theoretical and non-applicable if the culture does not support them. Strategy will always have to battle culture. It is a running battle that will never end. If the strategy is not aligned with and complemented by the existing organisational culture, it doesn't stand a chance. You will find sections of the workforce saying to themselves or, worse, saying to each other, things like, "We don't have such rules in this company," and, "That's not how we've always done things here," because that is what the prevailing culture has ingrained in them. Whatever strategies, action plans and rules have been documented become nothing more than theoretical. In this running culture-versus-strategy battle, there will only ever be one winner. To repeat the words of Peter Drucker, culture eats strategy for breakfast!

So, what does all this mean in the reality of corporate life? In answering this question, it is useful to revisit the conclusion I arrived at in Chapter 1: organisational culture is the common set of day-to-day behaviours, beliefs and expectations of all the people within an organisation regardless of what is formally documented.

This means that strategic objectives and plans, which will inevitably be formally documented, *must* be interrogated at the onset in order to establish whether or not they are complemented by the existing organisational culture. If the two are not aligned and mutually complementary, then all these wonderfully crafted and documented strategic objectives and action plans are reduced to conjecture. They may begin to come to fruition in the short-term due solely to fear, but will inevitably fall apart in the medium-to-long term.

We now begin to see the importance of establishing and understanding the cultural entropy and, with it, prevailing culture as the necessary starting point in any strategic planning session. In fact, the cultural entropy should be established well in advance, so that when strategy-setting and planning take place, the strategy-setters are working from an informed position where they can accurately forecast whether or not the strategic objectives and action plans can be properly and effectively implemented as things stand; or whether it is necessary to first embark on a culture-transformation exercise.

Another contributing factor in this running culture-versus-strategy battle, and the way it unfolds, is a common element of corporate culture which silently dictates that the business strategy and all things strategic are top-secret, and the preserve of the elite few. With that attitude and culture, effective implementation of strategic action plans becomes nigh on impossible. This particular issue is unpacked in more detail in the next chapter.

This culture-versus-strategy battle is a neverending one. This is a fact of business which, unfortunately, is seldom given the attention it deserves. Organisational culture is a living being that continuously grows and evolves, whether we like it or not. And this inevitable and unavoidable growth and evolution will either be in a direction that supports the strategy or hinders it.

Corporate culture is like a child, if you like. Whether the parents like it or not, their child will continuously grow, develop and change. It is the parents' job to keep nurturing that child in order to shape the growth as best as they can. They should feed that child the right food in order to support good physical growth, and they should provide the child the correct education and mental stimulation to support good intellectual growth. Whether they do these things or not, the child is still going to grow and develop in one way or another. And so, in the same vein, it is the job of business leaders to actively nurture the corporate culture as it grows and develops. What is perhaps most important to note is that the manner and direction in which the culture grows and evolves *can* be shaped, influenced and controlled if there is a deliberate emphasis on it.

It is the primary role of business leaders to continuously and deliberately assess the corporate culture and steer it in the direction that supports the strategy.

CHAPTER 4

"IT'S STRATEGIC!"

The strategy should be the business of everyone, not only of the select few!

This is a common go-to answer – "It's strategic!" – used by senior management when faced with a question that may, for want of a better term, be considered "tricky". We've all heard it before, and we all know its real meaning. It means that what you are asking is deemed too "high-level" or, to put it more accurately and certainly more bluntly, it is simply none of your business! This response invariably marks the end of the conversation.

I once brought up this very scenario in a management-training session, and the trainer's advice was that the retort to this common response ought to be, "Oh, which strategy is that?" This could only ever work in theory. In reality, where we live and work, "It's strategic!" is such a heavily loaded statement that anyone on the receiving end of it knows very well that a follow-up question is not an option.

Apart from putting an end to the discussion before it has even begun, this response illustrates a serious problem that is widely prevalent in the corporate world. Its clear implication is that the business strategy is the preserve of the select few. That all things strategic are neither of concern to, nor any business of, anyone other than those elite. And with this message, how is anyone outside this elite circle expected to meaningfully contribute to the fulfilment of strategic objectives?

This response engenders an organisational culture characterised by secrecy and division, which quickly leads to friction and frustration which, as we now know, increase the levels of cultural entropy. It engenders a culture where people are made to feel that asking questions is wrong. It engenders a culture where everyone outside the elite circle simply does their job and takes orders, often performing tasks without knowing why they are doing them in the first place. Worse, this sort of culture often leads to a situation where people performing certain tasks would, under different circumstances, be able to come up with different, better and more innovative ways of executing them, but the prevailing culture simply doesn't allow this. Yet, ironically, you will still find the people in this elite circle continually preaching about innovation – innovation which they are stifling and suffocating.

Ann Francke describes the situation very well when she says:

"[Strategy is often used] to confuse, threaten, condemn and otherwise torture colleagues. It is often a prelude for much complicated analysis and reams of PowerPoint slides and binders labelled 'strictly confidential'. The truth is, strategy is a set of simple choices, and relevant, interrelated and prioritised activities based on those choices."

This can be simplified even further:

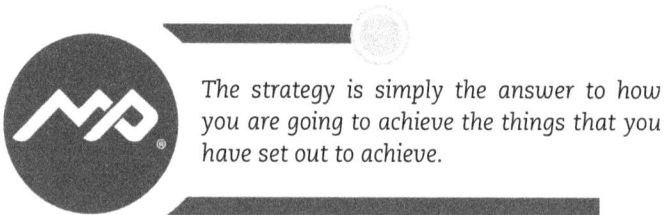

The strategy is simply the answer to how you are going to achieve the things that you have set out to achieve.

When looked at this way, it becomes abundantly clear that if the strategy is not everyone's business, you will inevitably have different people pulling in different directions, which is never going to give the desired outcome.

Different people within an organisation have different tasks and activities to perform. This is obvious. But each one must, surely, know the bigger picture behind those tasks and activities. If they don't, then there can be no common purpose or direction. This is when you have the infamous silo mentality. But the reality is that the people who exist in silos don't have any other option. Because when they attempt to remove themselves from these silos by asking questions in an attempt to understand the common purpose, they are quickly shut down and pushed back into their silo with one short, sharp and heavily loaded response: "It's strategic!" So, eventually there will be no further attempt to understand. And there will be a frustrated acceptance of this siloed existence.

Making the strategy a secret is a brilliant way of ensuring that it is not fulfilled. Strategic action plans cannot be implemented by people who don't know, let alone understand and buy into, the strategy itself. In his article, Freek Vermeulen shares a most apt quote from Sly Bailey who was, at the time, the CEO of the UK press publisher, Trinity Mirror: "*If there is one thing I have learned about communicating choices, it is that we always focus on what the choices are. I now realize you have to spend at least as much time on explaining the logic behind the choices.*"

In line with Chapter 3, the first step towards strategy implementation and fulfilment should be the conscious, deliberate and concerted effort to develop and engender a culture that supports the implementation of the strategy – *any* strategy.

A culture that supports strategy implementation cannot accommodate responses like, "It's strategic!"

CHAPTER 5

UNDERSTANDING

"Our actions can be no wiser than our thoughts. Our thoughts can be no wiser than our understanding."

This magical observation by George Clason is perhaps my favourite of all quotes. And if you take a step back and observe the goings-on around you, you can see this principle at play on a daily basis in most organisations. People get up and go to work, where they perform dozens of actions every day. These actions are in line with the thoughts of the person performing them. In line with what that person thinks he is supposed to be doing. In turn, what that person thinks he is supposed to be doing is either based on an understanding of his role and how it feeds into the bigger picture, or it is based on assumptions and guesswork with little or no understanding. If it is the latter, then actions are being performed mindlessly every day. What outcome can realistically be expected under such circumstances?

Understanding is, without doubt, the most critical element in anything you do. If you do not understand the aim, the goal or the objective, you will not achieve it – it's that simple. Understanding *is* the secret to success, in every aspect of life. In the context of this book, understanding is an essential element of business-strategy implementation, and it is a function of the organisational culture. As we have touched on, it is imperative that every person in an organisation knows what the strategy is, and what the strategic plan and related action steps are. But it is not good enough to simply *know* the strategy, the strategic plan and the action steps. You must *understand* them.

And so, a critical distinction begins to emerge – knowing versus understanding. This distinction is indispensable (or at least it should be), yet it is one that is seldom made. *Knowing* simply answers the question *what*. In the business context, it means that a person knows what his duties are. Understanding, on the other hand, goes much deeper. It entails asking and answering all the other questions, including *why*, *when*, *how*, and *who*. To put it another way, *knowing* is only a subset of *understanding*. This is illustrated in Figure 5.1.

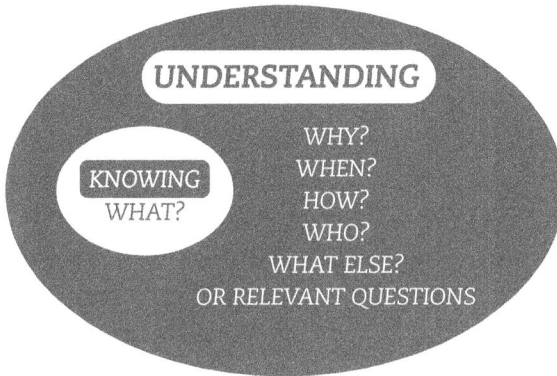

Figure 5.1: Knowing is a subset of understanding
Source: Pillay, M. (2019), *Life Demystified: Understanding – The Secret to Success*, Second Edition, p. 51

I like to call *why* "the king of questions". Because if you have clarity on the *why*, the other questions almost answer themselves.

In too many organisations, people routinely and mindlessly perform all sorts of activities every day. If you ask them why they are doing these things, you will be told, "Because my boss told me to," or, "Because that is what my job description says."

Many organisations talk about developing a culture of innovation. Innovation entails doing new things as well as doing the same things in a new and better way. To determine what new things can and should be done, and to determine what would constitute a better way of doing the same things, you have to have an understanding of those things.

This should be obvious. You have to be clear on why new things should be done; why they have not been done up to now; and why other things need to be done differently. In the absence of answers to these questions, you are just crossing your fingers, closing your eyes and hoping for the best.

Let us look at an easily identifiable real-life example of these principles at play. Take a floor-cleaner in a big store. This is, perhaps, the lowest level of employee (in terms purely of grading structures, nothing else), but even he should be able to tell you that over and above health and hygiene, the reason he is cleaning the floors of the store – the *why* – is because customers like to be in a clean environment; so if he keeps the floors clean the customers will keep coming back instead of going to the next store which is cleaner; and the company will make money. This is how he feeds into the growth strategy of the organisation. But the unfortunate reality is that only a very small percentage of cleaners will give you that answer. The majority will simply tell you that this is what they were hired to do, so they do it (mindlessly). In any organisation, for the effective implementation of its strategic goals, every person should not only feel comfortable, but also be encouraged to continue asking *why* they are doing certain things. This is where innovation begins.

From a place of clarity on the reason behind your actions, you become better equipped to deal with the other questions that must be asked and answered in order to arrive at this essential state of understanding: *how*, *who* and *when*, among others. Because ...

The reason determines the method and the timing.

Let's take the example further. How does the cleaner determine the best time to perform his tasks? The *when*, or the timing. He can only effectively do so when he is clear on why he is performing those tasks in the first place. The cleaner who doesn't know why he is cleaning the floors (other than because he was hired to do so) will perform this task at any random time, again, mindlessly. The timing is irrelevant and unimportant in his mind. But the cleaner who understands that he is performing this task for the benefit of the customers will then be in a position to further understand that customers don't want the inconvenience of having to negotiate their way around the cleaner and his utensils whilst doing their shopping. Equipped with this understanding, he will be able to make a decision to perform this task at a time when there are fewest customers.

Businesses are often governed by deadlines. Strategic goals always have timelines attached to them, and correctly so. This is entrenched by the

SMART goal-setting model which is widely used in business. In a nutshell, this model says that every goal should be Specific, Measurable, Assignable, Realistic, and Time-related. One of the many things that this model does *not* address is the basis for the timeframe. And the reality I have come to notice in the corporate environment is that timeframes are routinely set with no plausible basis. The primary basis is generally what looks good on the calendar. So, in management meetings you find business leaders boldly declaring things like, "We will launch new product X on the first of December," without considering all the inputs required, and how long each one is likely to take. If the same meeting was held two weeks earlier or two weeks later, you would probably still find the same launch date being set, simply because the first of December looks and sounds much better than the 16th of November or the 14th of December. The common result is that the deadline is not met, or product X is, indeed, launched on the first of December but it is substandard and turns out to be a flop. Or both! And this is because an impossible timeframe was set. And an impossible timeframe was set because it was not founded upon any understanding. It must be emphasised that timeframes and deadlines are good and necessary. But they *must* have a plausible basis. And that is understanding.

Another governing element in business is tracking and measuring. Again, correctly so. And this is also one of the elements of George T. Doran's

SMART model, which many businesses follow almost religiously. But I have come to notice a tendency for people to track and measure merely for the sake of ticking a box. This box that has been imposed by the SMART model. The result is that irrelevant metrics are tracked and measured but they mean very little in the grander scheme of things.

Once again, we must look at practical examples to illustrate and support this opinion. Businesses must continuously manage their costs to remain profitable. This is a fact. Manpower constitutes one of the major costs in any business, so it is not uncommon for human resources managers to be set goals like "reduce headcount by five within six months". And in many cases, you will get to the end of the six months, the headcount has indeed been cut by five and the normal wage bill reduced accordingly. The human resources manager gets a pat on the back and a positive performance review because the target has been met. But wait. On closer scrutiny (if one takes the time and has the insight to do so) it becomes apparent that other costs have increased significantly. Overtime has increased; after-hours allowances have increased; sundry costs have increased due to remaining staff working longer hours; consultancy charges have increased because certain tasks now need to be outsourced; and other staff have resigned as a result of the new, unrealistic workload, so recruitment charges have increased. There is also the business-continuity cost arising from these resignations. All these costs actually exceed what has been "saved" through the staff-headcount and wage-bill reduction. So, in a nutshell, the purpose of reducing the headcount – which was to reduce overall business costs – has not actually been achieved. But nobody will know this if the correct things are not measured. And the correct things will not be measured if there is no understanding.

I have touched on the SMART goal-setting model and some of its many shortcomings. Not only do I give a detailed critical analysis of it in *Life Demystified*, but I also share an alternative model for goal-setting which I developed. The UTMOST model is founded upon this critical element of any goal, *understanding*, and is summarised in Figure 5.2 on the following page.

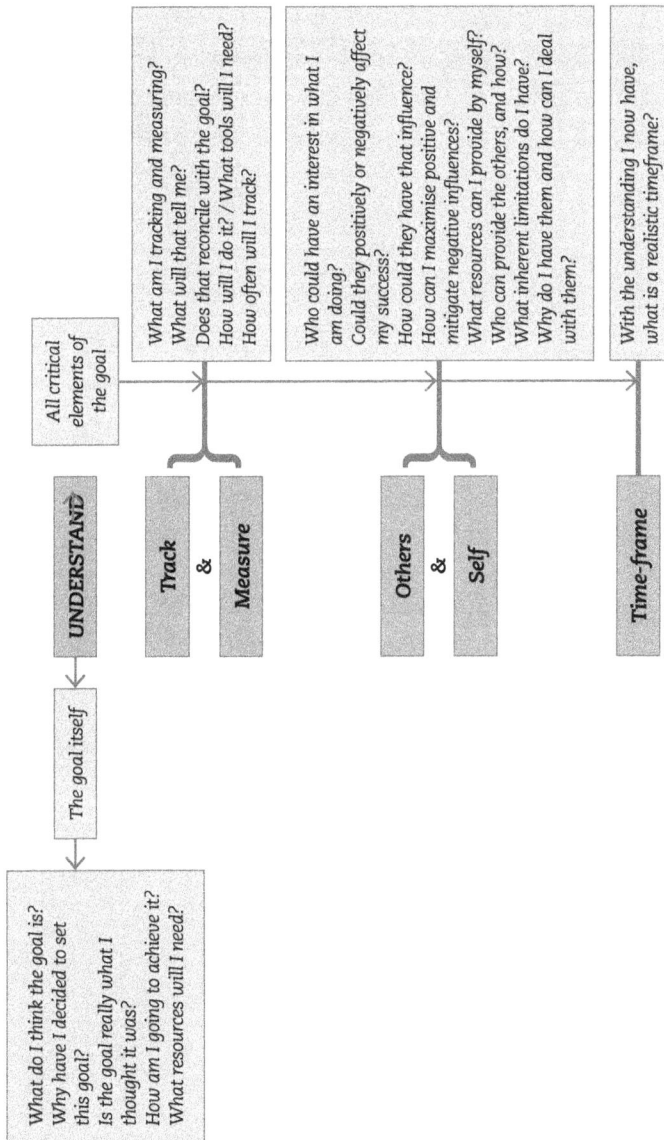

Figure 5.2: The UTMOST goal-setting model

Source: Pillay, M. (2019), *Life Demystified: Understanding – The Secret to Success*, Second Edition, p. 107

It is absolutely essential to engender a culture of understanding. And this can never be achieved as long as there are responses like, "It's strategic!"

Understanding is the state you arrive at when you know exactly what you are aiming to do, and have absolute clarity of why you are doing it, how you will do it, and when you will do it.

PART III
TIME

CHAPTER 6

TIME: ABUSED, UNDERVALUED AND DISRESPECTED

Time is the single most valuable resource any person and any organisation has. Bar none!

This is obviously a very strong statement, which requires justification. How can this single resource – time – be held in such high regard, above all the dozens, if not hundreds, of other resources that businesses make use of daily, weekly, monthly? Can time really be more valuable than that state-of-the-art, custom-made piece of machinery that was just purchased for over a million dollars? Can time really be more valuable than that multimillion-dollar bank balance?

You see, unlike any other resource, time can never be recovered or replaced. It is impossible! When machinery is damaged, it is possible to repair or replace it. When money is lost, it is possible to recover it. Even human resources can be and are routinely replaced. Admittedly, the replacement of these resources will, almost certainly, come at a financial cost; sometimes at a highly prohibitive cost which may render replacement highly unlikely in reality. Replacement, however, will always remain a possibility, even if not a probability. Time, on the other hand, stands in a league of its own, for it can never be replaced or recovered. It is, quite simply and quite literally, impossible! Over and above the fact that it can never be replaced, time is also most unique in the sense that while it is such an invaluable resource, it is, somehow, seldom recognised as a resource at all, let alone one that carries such value. The norm, rather, is that time is criminally undervalued, disrespected and abused.

I have come up with two logical conclusions for this. The first is that time is routinely wasted and abused without a second thought simply because it has no physical or *prima facie* monetary form. The second is that time is seen by many as a limitless resource. There are, of course, some more progressive organisations and business leaders that have begun to place a deliberate focus on work–life balance in recent times, and overall respect for personal time. In most organisations I have come across, however, it is quite the opposite. The mentality, which is created and entrenched by the corporate culture in these organisations, is that if a particular task is not completed within normal office hours, it matters not, because there are several more hours left in the day. The person in question will simply be expected to continue working on the task to completion, even if that means working until midnight or beyond. This is an aspect of organisational culture where all the focus is placed on money, with little value or respect for time and the people to whom that time belongs.

Time management is a term that is perhaps over-used, but seldom really implemented. It is worth recalling Professor Robert Kaplan's quote, which I shared in Chapter 2: "If you can't measure it, you can't manage it." In the context of this precious resource, I have found the need to slightly modify Kaplan's quote in line with my own observation that, not only in business but also in life generally, it is far more often a case of certain things not being measured by choice rather than because they can't be measured. So, I find it more apt to say:

If you don't measure it, you can't manage it.

This, I believe, highlights one of the biggest blind spots in business – the failure to track and measure the use of time. Not because they can't measure it, but rather because they choose not to. So, it is not just a failure, it is something worse. It is a refusal! The use of all other resources, from expensive raw materials down to 10-cent pens and pencils, is strictly tracked and measured yet, somehow, the use of time is excluded from these tracking and measuring exercises. If time is actively tracked and measured, then it can and will be managed in line with Kaplan's observation (as modified by me). But in the absence of any real tracking and measuring of time, the term "time management", no matter how often it is thrown about, is rendered meaningless. Where the corporate culture is such that time is a limitless resource, and the norm is that people can and will routinely work until midnight and beyond, then why should the use (and wastage) of time ever be measured? If four hours are wasted during the working day, and those four hours can and will be made up after hours, does it matter? This will inevitably raise the *en vogue* topic of flexitime, which I discuss in more detail in Chapter 8.

Another great quote comes from Johann Wolfgang von Goethe: "We always have time enough, if we will but use it aright." How true this is but, equally, how circumstantial it is. For this opinion is founded upon a very big assumption that every person has full control over the way they use their time. In a similar vein, Brian Tracy tells us that time management is essentially life management. That it is simply taking control of the sequence of events and what we do next. Again, this is founded upon the assumption that every person has the power to take that control. It fails to take account of the numerous interruptions that are the order of the day in many organisations (we will look at interruptions in more detail in Chapter 9).

Many people do, indeed, try to "use their time aright" and take control of their sequence of events. But how often do we find daily and weekly plans being consigned to the dustbin because something suddenly needs urgent attention? And it is not only these plans that are consigned to the dustbin, but the precious time that was spent making them as well. Time that can never be recovered. The unfortunate reality is that the latter seldom gets a thought. And this sort of thing keeps happening and, before you know it, urgency has become the norm rather than the exception. Urgency becomes part of the corporate culture, which we look at in more detail in the next chapter. And it will keep happening as a matter of culture because the person responsible for creating an unnecessarily "urgent" situation does so in the knowledge that someone else will have to, and will, drop everything to tidy up the urgent mess. This is a very clear indication that there is little respect for people's time, and a very strong implication that the time of the person having to drop everything in the name of urgency, is seen as less important than the time of the person who has created and declared this urgency.

You see, it is one thing to take all possible steps to ensure that you are using your time wisely, and not wasting it. But it is something quite different having to try and avoid *somebody else* wasting *your* time. It is an unfortunate reality of the corporate world, but one which is seldom, if ever, mentioned. Despite the circumstantial and theoretical guidance routinely given by time-management coaches, trainers and commentators, one can never take control of their time and effectively manage it unless and until the organisational culture not only allows it, but also facilitates it.

Interruptions – whether in the name of urgency or not – are a plague in business! According to Edward Brown as recounted by Brigid Schulte, interruptions account for the wastage of 40–60 percent of workers' time. If the use of time was simply tracked and measured along with the other resources used by a business, things might be different. But to repeat, somehow, time is generally deemed unworthy of tracking and measuring. And this failure and refusal to measure the use of time leads to routine abuse: abuse of time and the simultaneous, consequential abuse of the people to whom the time belongs. To reiterate, where the corporate culture is such that working ridiculous hours is expected and normal, then there is really no need to track and measure the use of people's time during office hours because, by virtue of the culture, all 24 hours in a day are *de facto* office hours. If 40–60 percent (which equates to three to five hours per eight-office-hour day) of workers' time is wasted, it means little when there are still another 16 hours in a 24-hour day to make up this wasted time.

Let us remind ourselves of a few things. Time does not exist in a vacuum. Time belongs to people, and each person should, ideally, be responsible and accountable for their own time. Every person has the same number of hours in a day. The time of one person, therefore, can never be more important than the time of another person. It is, of course, an undeniable fact of the corporate world that the higher your paygrade, the more *valuable* your time. But it comes with a strict qualification that is rarely, if ever, mentioned. Probably by design rather than omission! This qualification is that the proportional relationship between a person's paygrade and the value of their time *applies only to office hours*. The personal time of one person can never be more valuable than the personal time of another, regardless of job titles and paygrades. The hour spent by the CEO with his new baby after work is no more valuable than the hour spent by the floor-cleaner with his own new baby. Failure or refusal to recognise this betrays a gross disrespect not only for a person's time, but for the person himself.

Going further, the *value* of one's time during office hours should also not be confused with the *importance* of one's time. Every person in an organisation, from top- to bottom-graded employees, has his key performance indicators, critical tasks and expected outputs which he is expected to achieve through efficient and effective use of his time. Each person's output in an organisation constitutes a vital cog in the organisational machinery. Without any one of these cogs, the organisation cannot achieve its overall outputs optimally or at all. By that reasoning, every person's time must carry equal importance and must be equally respected.

In many organisations the corporate culture is such that people are expected to, and do, effectively give away their personal time to the organisation. It is a clear, and sometimes even written, expectation. Organisations would never dream of asking employees to donate a portion of their personal finances to cover its financial losses incurred through poor management, yet that is exactly the expectation when it comes to time. This is because time is not recognised as the finite and precious resource it really is and, therefore, continues to be grossly abused.

Time is inseparable from people. If you genuinely value and respect a person, you must equally value and respect the time of that person.

CHAPTER 7

"IT'S URGENT!"

There is a serious problem when urgency becomes the norm rather than the exception.

These two words, "it's urgent", have the ability to send shivers down the spine of many who work in the corporate world. On the face of things, these are just two short words. But if you look deeper, there is much more to them. In the corporate world, when someone in a more senior position to you declares, "It's urgent!" the real messages that are being conveyed include, *"Immediately drop everything you're doing; you'll be here until late tonight; and if this is not completed there will be serious consequences."*

There is no doubt that urgent matters are an unavoidable reality of doing business and they must be treated and dealt with accordingly. But, to repeat, the problem arises when urgency becomes the norm rather than the exception.

Before I go any further, I should perhaps highlight one very important principle which, quite surprisingly, seems to escape many business people. If a task is urgent, it means that something has gone wrong somewhere along the process flow. Something has happened that is contrary to what normal business processes and procedures dictate should happen. And so, I repeat, urgent matters will inevitably crop up from time to time but, most critically, this should be the exception rather than the rule. If urgency becomes the rule and the norm, it means that things are routinely going wrong in the process flow, and nothing is being done to address the real problem that is causing things to routinely go wrong. It could even be that the process flow, itself, is not fit for purpose and needs to be revised. If urgency has become the norm, it means that the organisational culture is such that is it is okay to keep letting things go wrong. The organisational culture is such that when things go wrong, we will simply drop what we are doing, as a matter of routine, and take the urgent action required to cover up the thing that has gone wrong, instead of trying to get to the root of the problem.

I began my career as a young attorney in private practice. Here, I was irreversibly shaped and moulded on the issue of urgency, and necessarily so. You see, in the legal profession, there are very clear and very stringent rules and requirements which *must* be satisfied in order for one to approach a court of law for urgent relief. Any attorney will attest to the daunting nature of the task of first having to try and convince a judge that the matter is genuinely urgent, before even being afforded the opportunity to argue the merits of the case.

One of the requirements is that the litigant seeking urgent relief must approach the courts *immediately* upon coming to learn of the circumstances that warrant this urgent action. If a litigant approaches the courts for urgent relief weeks or, in some cases, even days after becoming aware of the situation at hand, the courts will simply not entertain it on an urgent basis. It will be categorised as self-created urgency – a category with which a court of law will not involve itself. In a nutshell, the judge is effectively saying that he will not allow himself to be unnecessarily put under pressure because of the litigant's tardiness and carelessness, and that the litigant must now deal with, and be accountable for, the consequences of his failure to act on time.

Over and above the stringent requirements imposed by the courts, attorneys are permitted to charge hefty premiums on their normal fee. The primary purpose of this is to properly compensate an attorney for having to drop everything else, and to work abnormal hours due to this urgency. But it also serves the purpose – perhaps inadvertently – of making a client think twice and think objectively before running to his attorney with this problem and declaring, "It's urgent!"

So, what we have in the legal profession is a universal and objective understanding, appre-ciation and acceptance of the meaning and implications of this declaration, "It's urgent!"

The corporate world, sadly, is quite the opposite. There are generally no universally accepted rules, understandings or appreciations of what is urgent. If there are, they certainly have no objective and logical basis. There are no accepted requirements for what should be dealt with as urgent, and what should not. There is little or no interrogation into whether this issue has just come to light, or whether someone has been sitting on it for a week, or two or ten. And there is generally no effort to avoid a repeat. After all, why should person A avoid repeating his error when he knows that he will not be held accountable, and that person B will simply deal with it, urgently, when it happens again the next time?

The one rule, albeit unwritten, that has seemingly gained universal acceptance in the corporate world when it comes to urgency, is that the more senior the person making this dreaded pronouncement – "It's urgent!" – the more "urgent" it becomes. And this is a product purely of the organisational culture. Unlike the judge who refuses to be put under pressure which has been unnecessarily created by the litigant's failure to act timeously, corporate culture often dictates that the person further along the process flow must silently and routinely accept the pressure caused by someone else's failures earlier on in the process flow. And, unlike the attorney who brings this urgent case before the judge, there is no financial (or other) reward for the employee who is delegated the task of sorting out urgent matters handed down to him.

I have found that in any aspect of life, anything that one does not pay for is generally abused. So, it becomes a culture of routine abuse of the people who are continually having to drop what they are doing to deal with ad hoc "urgent" tasks and the pressure that they bring. It is a culture that not only lacks any real accountability, but one that actually promotes total disregard for accountability where it should lie. Accountability, almost magically, seems to shift from where it should lie – i.e. with the person who has caused this urgency to arise – to the person who is now having to tidy it up. This is a culture that dictates that it is okay to *not* do your part on time, because the next person will take care of it. Attempts are often made, wrongly, to justify this undesirable state of affairs in the name of teamwork, which is discussed in detail in Chapter 16.

Any elementary management book or course will almost invariably contain a section which highlights the importance of saying, "No", and of occasionally letting things fail in the short-term, for the benefit the lesson in the failure will bring in the long-term. And this is precisely what happens in the legal profession. Some may wonder what the value of letting things fail is. You see, if things are covered up through continual urgent action, no red flag is raised and nothing changes. But if something fails, someone will be answerable. It promotes accountability and it promotes a culture of continuous improvement. It makes all the sense in the world because, to repeat yet again:

If something has become urgent it means that something has gone wrong and the normal processes cannot now be followed.

In other words, the urgency is and should be recognised as a symptom of a real problem. And if this keeps happening, and then keeps getting covered up through urgent action somewhere further along the process flow, you are only temporarily remedying one symptom of the problem rather than treating the problem itself. The real problem that has created this urgency will never be remedied. All this is consistent with the age-old adage, "We learn from our mistakes." But as long as this urgent cover-up routine remains the norm, there is no acknowledgement or even realisation that there was a mistake at all. And if there is no acknowledgement that a mistake was made, there can be no learning from it.

But the importance of saying, "No", as preached by management commentators and trainers, is – as with many other principles we have looked at – merely idealistic. It assumes that managers are actually managing and are empowered to do so by the leadership, rather than being reduced to doers of ad hoc, urgent tasks. Personal and business success guru, Brian Tracy, tells us of the importance of planning your day in advance, at the end of the previous day. This, Tracy says, serves two major purposes – first, it will allow you to get straight into action when the new day begins; and, second, it allows your subconscious mind to begin, today, working on tomorrow's tasks. But what actual value does this theoretically good advice have when, in reality, your daily plans are routinely discarded because you are met with a totally new task, and it's *urgent!?*

In reality, we find many businesses continuing to pursue this mythical creature called business efficiencies, which we look at in more detail in Chapter 10. Yet the situation on the ground, shaped by the organisational culture, says something completely different. Unless and until "urgency" is properly interrogated when it raises its head, and things are occasionally allowed to fail, the culture is entrenched as one in which urgency is the norm. And when urgency is the norm, plans are routinely discarded to accommodate the latest urgent issue and adhocracy will inevitably prevail! In the coming chapters, we will look at how this dreaded culture of urgency negatively impacts an organisation in so many different contexts.

The normalisation of urgent action serves only to perpetuate something that is going wrong, and to divert accountability.

CHAPTER 8

FLEXITIME: FRIEND OR FOE?

Flexitime is a tool – nothing more, nothing less!

This is the necessary starting point when we talk about flexitime. So much so, that it is worth immediately repeating and emphasising it. Flexitime is, quite simply, a tool!

Every tool, in every facet of life, was created to fulfil a specific purpose and to achieve a specific outcome. Every tool was designed to be used in a certain way that will facilitate the outcome for which it was designed. So, against this backdrop, it follows that if a tool is used in a way and/or to achieve a purpose other than that for which it was specifically designed, then the value of that tool decreases significantly, to the extent that the tool can actually become a hazard.

To illustrate what I'm saying, let us look

at a common tool which fits the conventional understanding of this word "tool", and with which everyone is familiar – a simple spanner. A spanner is designed specifically to tighten/loosen nuts. It is designed in such a way that it fits the nut perfectly (or vice versa), and gives the user the required leverage to effectively tighten/loosen the nut. When used for its specific purpose and in the correct manner, the spanner works like a charm. It is a valuable tool. It is your friend.

Now, I'm pretty sure that I can't be the only person who has seen a spanner being used for other purposes, such as hammering nails when a hammer is not readily available. A hammer is a different tool altogether, and designed specifically for use in hammering nails. It has distinctly diffe-rent features to a spanner. When a spanner is used to achieve the hammer's purpose, common results – arising from the unsuitable design of the spanner – include nails not being straight; consequent poor-quality workmanship; and injury to the user due to a largely predictable slip of the spanner in the process of hammering. In a nutshell, the spanner is your friend when used properly, but very quickly becomes your foe when not used properly. Because flexitime is nothing more than a tool, all of the above similarly applies. Flexitime is your business spanner, if you like.

Applying my own logic and common sense, and leveraging my own experience in the corporate world, I believe that there are – or at least should be – two founding principles of flexitime: trust and purpose.

Trust

Flexitime, first and foremost, is founded upon trust. The people who make use of this tool – flexitime – must be trusted to use it properly. If there is no inherent trust, this tool serves no positive purpose.

I have seen and even been involved in situations where flexitime has been spoken about at length in strategic planning sessions, and followed through with the careful crafting of policy and procedure documents. Unfortunately, these documents ultimately become academic because there is no trust that this tool will be used properly.

You find questions being asked by the business leaders – the same people who sanctioned the introduction of this tool in the first place – such as: "How do we know that people will not abuse it? How do we know that people will not work fewer hours than they are supposed to?"

The simple and obvious answer to these questions is, "Trust the people!"

Trust is a key element of corporate culture in general. And when questions of this nature are asked, it reveals a lot about the culture. It reveals a culture that lacks trust. If there is no trust, it necessarily means that there is an underlying assumption that the tool will be abused or misused. That employees will use this tool to get away with working fewer hours than they should.

There is an assumption that the spanner will be used as a hammer. As a result, the people who are supposed to use this tool will not be allowed to do so or, alternatively, they will be unduly monitored as they use it. In the latter case, a paradox begins to unfold. You see, the purpose of flexitime, which is expanded upon later, is to increase efficiency. But what is happening in reality is that the people who are using this tool for its intended purpose are not trusted. And because they are not trusted, they are being monitored as they use this tool. Consequently, the people doing the monitoring have become less efficient in their own duties because they are wasting valuable time monitoring others who they shouldn't be monitoring and wouldn't be monitoring if there was any meaningful level of trust. So, any efficiency gained by those using the flexitime tool, is simultaneously lost by those monitoring them as they use it.

While we're on the topic of trust, it is perhaps an opportune time to highlight that trust is very closely linked to another critical element of the corporate culture – empowerment. I could go as far as saying that trust is the parent of empowerment. Empowerment cannot exist without trust. If staff are not genuinely empowered to make decisions about the most effective and efficient use of their time, then similarly, flexitime is pointless.

Purpose

To go back to the overarching principle in *Life Demystified*, before you embark on something, it is critical to ask the king of questions – *why*. By asking and answering this question, you will establish the purpose of, or reason for, your actions.

The primary purpose of flexitime is to maximise efficiency, with a particular focus on the use of time – our most precious resource. The effective use of this tool allows people to complete the tasks they need to complete in the shortest possible time. Flexitime is concerned with reducing time wastage and, as always, it is important to look at real examples to illustrate this.

A common feature of flexitime is to allow people to begin and end work, as a rule of thumb, an hour either side of normal office hours. So, if office hours are 8am to 5pm, one is given the flexibility to work 7am to 4pm, or 9am to 6pm instead.

To repeat, flexitime is concerned with reducing time wasted. Every country has got what is known as peak traffic hours. In Zimbabwe, where I have spent my entire career thus far, those peak hours are generally 7am to 8am, and 4.30pm to 5.30pm. During these peak hours, a 10km drive to or from the office can easily take an hour. That means two hours per day spent driving and, in the process, two hours of doing nothing productive.

If instead one drives to and from the office outside these peak hours, the same 10km journey takes 15 minutes. Applying simple arithmetic, this equates to 45 minutes saved each way. That is one and a half hours per day and over 30 hours per month saved, simply by changing the time that you commute.

The secondary purpose of flexitime is to enhance work–life balance. Because let's face it, work is but one of many facets of life, and it should never be the most important aspect of anybody's life. Life continues to happen regardless of work hours and work commitments, and if you're not careful and not mindful of this, you will miss out on large and invaluable chunks of life. Social functions; school meetings; kids' concerts; having an extended lunch with an old friend who is in town for a couple days; and general personal commitments – these all happen. Flexitime allows you to attend to these commitments whilst still putting in the requisite hours and, perhaps more importantly, producing the required output as far as work commitments go.

Now that we are clear on what the purpose of flexitime is, it is equally important to talk about what the purpose of flexitime is *not*. And on that note, I'd like to revisit a passage from Chapter 6: "*Where the corporate culture is such that time is a limitless resource, and the norm is that people can and will routinely work until midnight and beyond, why should the use (and wastage) of time ever be measured? If four hours are wasted, and those four hours can and will be made up after hours, does it matter?*"

I'm a sports fanatic. And with the popularity and prevalence of sport in modern society, I'm quite certain that a large proportion of readers will easily identify with sports analogies. So, before I unpack the above passage, I'd like to introduce one such analogy.

If you've ever watched a soccer match, you will have almost invariably seen the team managers making substitutions as the game goes on. Actually, this applies to most if not all team sports. One player comes into the game to replace another who has not been effective. The in-coming player does not increase the numbers. The number of players on the field remains the same. The substitution is made so that the same number of players can work towards the defined goal in a more effective manner than they were prior to the substitution. Flexitime is the workplace equivalent. It allows a person to be the manager of his time – to remove ineffective and inefficient hours from his workday, and replace them with more effective ones. The purpose is *not* to add extra hours onto the workday.

So, to get back to the passage from Chapter 6, the purpose of flexitime is also *not* to make up hours lost to interruptions in the workplace – a plague that I discuss in detail in the next chapter. The reality in many organisations, however, is that flexitime is a ruse. Business leaders use it to coerce staff into working additional hours; to provide a platform which allows business leaders to make unfair demands on people's personal time; and, in general, to legitimise and justify abnormal working hours.

There is, of course, a more appropriate tool to achieve these purposes. It is called overtime. But overtime presents a problem – it comes with a monetary cost to the business. So, to avoid this monetary cost, you find flexitime being used to try and achieve the purpose for which overtime was created. Flexitime becomes the spanner being used to hammer nails. The tool becomes a foe rather than a friend and, importantly, it again betrays a culture where people and their time are disrespected and abused in the name of maximising profits.

And this is where the paradox becomes most evident. Business leaders who unduly monitor their staff because they don't trust them to use flexitime properly, are the people most guilty of misusing and abusing flexitime!

If the purpose is not to genuinely trust and empower staff to manage their time in order to make the most effective and efficient use of it, then flexitime will always be a foe, never a friend.

CHAPTER 9

INTERRUPTIONS: THE UNSEEN PLAGUE

"Procrastination is the thief of time"... so the saying goes. I hold a different view.

The real thief of time, and a plague that wreaks havoc in the business world, is interruptions.

How often do you get interrupted during a typical day at the office? How long does it then take you to retrace your mental steps and thought process after each interruption, simply to get yourself, mentally, back to the place you left off? How much of your time is therefore wasted by these interruptions? Most of us probably can't answer this question with any level of accuracy because our time, and particularly its wastage through interruptions, is never tracked and measured in any meaningful manner, or at all. Fortunately, several studies have been conducted that can help us answer this question with some degree of accuracy.

In many organisations, interruptions – apart from being a plague – have become the elephant in the room. They loom large, but people don't talk about them when it's time to talk about serious issues. If they get a mention, it is in passing and often with a generous helping of jest to accompany it. Business executives preach this ridiculous "open-door" gospel and then immediately retreat to the safety and seclusion of their ivory towers, which are diligently manned by their no-nonsense PAs. They have a vague idea of the interruptions going on amongst the masses, but choose to turn a blind eye, thus exonerating themselves of any duty to fix it. In many cases, these executives are actually among the worst culprits or, as some say, the worst time-bandits. This is not surprising given the common attitude that the time of people at a lower level is less valuable and seen as less important (as discussed in Chapter 6). And so, the culture of time wasting continues to entrench itself.

I have read countless articles on interruptions in the workplace. Without exception, they mention the fact that office workers always complain about this aspect. But these complaints are invariably directed at the person writing the article, or a person who conducted some study which is referred to. The complaints will not be directed at the people who can actually do something about it. This is because the culture accepts these interruptions, and entrenches them through catchphrases like "open-door policy", "teamwork", and "internal customer service", among others. This makes it impossible for a person to speak up about the constant interruptions, because it will lead to only one thing – that person being labelled as uncooperative, stubborn, and generally difficult. That person who chooses to point out the elephant in the room is very quickly seen as someone who has created a problem in the organisation rather than someone who has pointed out the existence of a serious problem that needs to be solved. It brings us back to a culture of fear.

Many of these articles about interruptions go on to suggest possible "solutions" to this plague. These include, among others: time-blocking; retreating to private places; and developing "do-not-disturb" indicators. Surely the better option is to take the bull by the horns, and openly address this recurring problem? This plague! Theoretically, yes. But where the culture does not encourage or even allow people to speak openly and honestly about these constant interruptions, many workers do, indeed, make use of these "solutions" as the next best option. You find people hiding in meeting rooms and training rooms in a desperate attempt to escape the constant interruptions. People can even be found going to such extremes as taking their laptops and going to work in their cars. Not only have I personally observed co-workers resorting to these drastic measures, I have also employed them myself! And each time I've done so, I've thought to myself, "Surely this is not normal!?" But here's the thing: in many organisations, it is normal because, to reiterate, the corporate culture has normalised it!

In one instance, I hatched a brilliant plan with one of my colleagues. We booked a meeting room for the whole morning, ostensibly to discuss a very important and confidential issue. We were both at senior-middle-management level, each of us heading a department, so this didn't raise any eyebrows. For the whole morning, we each got on with what we needed to do, not breathing a word to each other. What a productive morning!

The first problem I have with these "solutions" is that they serve only to perpetuate the plague. They do not solve the problem, but merely cover it up temporarily. They are ways of dealing with what is seen as inevitable rather than trying, instead, to eliminate the inevitability of these interruptions so that workers don't have to focus their energies on devising all sorts of outlandish plans simply to be able to do their work properly and productively. These "solutions" are tacit acceptance that constant interruptions are normal and inevitable. Just like urgency, the norm is to address the symptom rather than solving the real problem giving rise to the symptom.

The second problem I have is that many of these "solutions" are highly theoretical, taking little or no account of the reality of the typical work environment; the way co-workers and superiors think and behave; corporate politics; and, on the whole, the prevailing organisational culture. These are the *real* considerations.

Theoretically, you can use a "do-not-disturb" indication. Theoretically, you can time-block – deferring emails and telephone calls that come in during that window. The reality, however, is that sooner or later you will find co-workers complaining and reporting to their bosses that you are inaccessible and are holding things up. This will be exacerbated in an organisation with a culture of urgency, which we discussed in Chapter 7. That co-worker's boss will escalate further until, just like the outcome of speaking openly about these interruptions in the first place, the overall picture that is painted is that you are uncooperative, you are not a team player etc. So, workers simply suffer in silence. And they become disgruntled, disengaged and generally unhappy.

Let's get on to some of the studies that have been conducted into this plague that continues to bedevil workers and businesses. The one that has seemingly gained the most popularity in recent years is the study conducted by Gloria Mark in 2008, which is nicely supplemented by an interview she later did with Kermit Patterson. Gloria Mark's key findings include the following:

- Workers are interrupted, on average, every 10.5 minutes; and
- It takes the interrupted person an average of 23 minutes and 15 seconds to get back to where

they left off.

Of course, these findings cannot be applied across the board. They must be contextualised and there must be an appreciation of the existence of so many variables. Gloria Mark, herself, does give a qualification to the effect that the extent of the time lost will depend on the type of interruption. I would extend this to take account of the type of work being done at the time of the interruption.

A Loughborough University study is another worth looking into. This study focused on email interruptions, which it found to take an average of 64 seconds to recover from. The study also observed that it takes even longer to recover after being interrupted by a telephone call. This demonstrates that, just like the findings of Gloria Mark's study, this is obviously highly circumstantial and subject to certain qualifications.

Notwithstanding the qualifications and contextualisation that need to be applied, and the inherent variables, what we now have – which was my primary objective in looking at these studies – is an evidence-based range. A range of average time periods it takes a person to recover from each interruption. In other words, how much time is wasted by each interruption on average. This ranges from 64 seconds to 23 minutes and 15 seconds. For purposes of convenience, we will work with a range of 1 minute to 23 minutes.

I once had a CEO whose standard response to

almost everything was, "Show me the numbers." Notwithstanding my less-than-favourable opinion on such a response, this is one instance where I believe it is, indeed, vital to "show you the numbers". If we use Gloria Mark's finding that on average, a person is interrupted every 10.5 minutes, that equates to 45 interruptions in an eight-hour day, which further translates to about 1 000 interruptions per person per month.

Now let's apply the average time wasted per interruption (remember, the range is 1 minute to 23 minutes) to this average number of interruptions (which is 1 000 interruptions per person per month). This means that your average organisation has between 1 000 minutes (17 hours) and 23 000 minutes (383 hours) of each person's time wasted every month through interruptions. I shall not attempt to critique Gloria Mark's findings. Suffice to say, it is my unsubstantiated opinion that 383 hours per month seems quite far-fetched and unrealistic, but certainly worth being aware of. As such, the realistic conclusion is that, on average, every organisation is experiencing a time wastage of at least 17 hours per person per month! Pause, and think about that.

If each interruption translated to a loss of 60 dollars or 60 units of stock instead of 60 seconds, would these interruptions be accepted as the norm? Would business leaders continue to turn a blind eye to this ever-growing elephant in the room? Obviously not. They would be tracked and measured religiously, and reduced very quickly!

It must be reiterated and emphasised that this pandemic is squarely a function of the culture. And in order to truly rid itself of this plague, every organisation needs its leaders to take a more deliberate approach to time management. Time management means time measurement and, with it, wasted-time measurement. To repeat, if you don't measure it, you can't manage it. Simple!

As long as the use of time, in particular its wastage, is not actively tracked and measured, it will remain the invaluable yet unvalued and abused resource.

Give yourself the *real* competitive advantage

PART IV
BUSINESS
EFFICIENCIES

CHAPTER 10

THE MYTH OF BUSINESS EFFICIENCIES

The Oxford English Dictionary provides a great starting point:

"efficient: preventing the wasteful use of a particular resource."

Despite this simple and to-the-point definition, business efficiencies are often made out to be some sort of mythical, almost unattainable, holy grail in the corporate world. This culminates in business efficiencies being discussed as a high-level strategic objective, with a considerable number of hours, if not days, being devoted to the topic – devising plans, actions, activities, processes, policies and procedures all aimed at trying to attain this mythical holy grail.

The reality is that business efficiencies, despite

the mythical status often attached to them, are largely simple and straightforward matters of general observation, logic and common sense. They are, by no means, the myth or strategic conundrums that they are often portrayed to be.

Indeed, formal business processes and procedures have their place and are necessary, but only to some extent. I focus on these in Chapter 12. There cannot be, and certainly should not be, a formal process or procedure for every single task that is performed, or action that is taken on a day-to-day basis. This is why we hire good managers and good staff. They must exercise their discretion and logic to make decisions that they believe are good for business and that generally make the most sense under the prevailing circumstances. I am firmly of the view that the majority of business inefficiencies fall outside formal processes and procedures. This chapter aims to substantiate that opinion.

If we go back to the definition above, we see that business efficiencies are simply ways of doing things that prevent or minimise the wastage of business resources. And these resources can be any number of things, including money, energy, materials and most importantly, time. I must reiterate that in my experience, the most rampant of inefficiencies in business relate to the wastage of one particular resource – time. Part III covered this extensively.

How often have you received an email from a

colleague, and within 30 seconds, your telephone extension rings and it is that very same colleague calling to say, "I sent you an email." *Erm … okay.* Unless that statement is immediately followed by something like, "It is extremely urgent, so I would be grateful if you could make this a priority," then what on earth is that call achieving or supposed to be achieving?

Some organisations have formal communication policies and procedures which would set out what should be done with regard to emails, and when these things should be done. But, more importantly, whether these formal policies exist or not, logic and common sense tell us (or should tell us) a number of things, including:

- That the recipient of this email – or any email – will not be attending to and responding to emails at every minute of every day because they have other tasks to perform;
- That the recipient will, at some point, see the email and send an initial response within a reasonable and acceptable time period, which is normally 24 hours; and
- That the initial response will either address the issue raised, or will acknowledge receipt and give an indicative timeframe for a more substantive response.

All this is common sense and common business etiquette. Or at least it should be! When these things do not happen, and when email-senders are making follow-up calls within seconds of hitting the "send" button, simply to say, "I sent you an email," it is not because of the existence or non-existence of policies and procedures to optimise business efficiencies. It is because of the organisational culture. And there are a number of different factors that could define the corporate culture in this context. I have picked out two. It may be that there is a lack of trust in technology. There is some level of doubt that emails are getting to their intended destination, which presents the need to confirm this through a phone call. (Yes, there are still people who fall into this category, believe it or not!) Alternatively, it may be that the sender of the email, knowing the culture of this particular organisation, thinks to himself, "I may never get a response to my email, despite the fact that I know it was received and despite the communication policy that is in place. So, I'd better follow up with a phone call, otherwise nothing will happen." The latter, I have found, is the most rampant. I call it the curse of follow-ups.

Let's look at this curse further. In any organisation and in any process, all major outputs require a number of different inputs from a number of different people. The assumption is that each person knows not only what their respective inputs are, but also the expected timing of those inputs. And in my experience this is, indeed, the case. People generally *do* know what they are supposed to be doing and when they are supposed to be doing it, whether or not it is formally documented. But despite this knowledge, far too many simply do not do those things until they are followed up. So, going back to the phone call immediately after an email is sent ... This is, effectively, the first of many follow-ups that the email-sender *knows* he has to make in order to get the thing done.

This is the unfortunate reality. People know that if they don't continually make these follow-ups, nothing will be done on time and things will, sooner or later, become urgent. And, worse, the wrong person is held accountable. This has become the order of the day in many businesses. Weekly and monthly reports, status updates and dashboards are churned out, routinely reflecting statements like, "To follow up with Mr X." And the people receiving these reports routinely accept this as the norm. This is partially a manifestation of another syndrome I look into in Chapter 13 – when managers don't manage!

Let us be clear on one thing: if there is any follow-up having to be made, it is because someone has simply not done what they were supposed to do, and has not bothered to say so either.

Indeed, there are genuine cases where sudden, unexpected events disrupt our plans, making it nigh on impossible to meet certain deadlines. It happens! But there is still a duty to communicate to the next person that you will not meet the initial deadline, and to simultaneously propose a new one. Perhaps the most important aspect of this duty is that you should perform it before someone has had to make a follow-up when you've missed the deadline. And this duty arises not from policy or procedure, but from common sense, common courtesy and general business etiquette. The fact that this is not done and that the follow-up must be, and is, made – as a matter of routine in most cases – talks not to policies and procedures. It talks primarily to the organisational culture.

To reiterate, follow-ups are one of the biggest curses faced by businesses. Follow-ups account for a large proportion of interruptions in the workplace – a plague that we looked at in Chapter 9. They serve only to expose the fact that people are simply not doing what they know they should be doing, when they should be doing it. And each follow-up is an unproductive use of the time of both the person following up and the person being followed up. In the previous chapter we looked, in detail, at how much time is actually wasted on interruptions. But follow-ups become the norm because the organisational culture dictates that it is okay *not* to do things on time and, also, not to say anything about it either. The organisational culture is one that lacks respect for co-workers, and lacks accountability for things that are not done when they are supposed to be done.

Before thinking about high-level strategic plans and devising a plethora of policies and procedures aimed at optimising business efficiencies, a bit of time needs to be taken to analyse how routine day-to-day activities are carried out, which is a function of the corporate culture more than anything else.

Work on developing a culture where people are, quite simply, doing the things they know they are supposed to be doing, when they are supposed to be doing them, or communicating when they cannot. It's that simple!

CHAPTER II

WORK SMART, NOT HARD!

Synonymous with this myth called business efficiencies, discussed in Chapter 10, is the *en vogue* term that gets bandied about by business leaders with increasing frequency: "Work smart". As much as the term is used, there appears to be little real appreciation for what it actually means, and how one can "work smart" in reality. It makes sense, then, to try and unpack this term before going any further. In a nutshell, it means reducing the time you use and the energy you exert without compromising on the output.

> *Working smart talks to the route you choose to take to arrive at the same defined destination.*

With this understanding, it becomes easy to see how working smart is synonymous with business efficiencies. Both concepts focus on reducing the wastage of resources. You could go as far as saying that working smart is a subset of business efficiencies. A subset that is focused on the wise and effective use of the most important resource – time.

Working smart means arriving at work, identifying your key tasks for the day, prioritising them, doing what you need to do in a way that takes up the least amount of your time and energy, and then quickly moving on to the next key task. Tools that help people to work smarter include planning (and sticking to the plan), technology, and delegation. We begin to see, then, that working smart is closely linked to innovation. If you want to work smarter, you must necessarily be innovative in the ways you complete your tasks.

We all like to tell ourselves that we are working smarter or, at least, that we should be working smarter rather than working harder. But the reality of the corporate world is such that you cannot and will not work smarter unless the culture allows you to. And, of course, until you understand what it means. We have already looked at how the culture in many organisations doesn't allow effective planning, and how there is sometimes a lack of trust in technology. Let's take a look at delegation, which is the other enabling tool that I've specifically mentioned.

I was once assigned a legal graduate trainee to work under me. In this organisation, one of the contract documents we used for our business partners accounted for over 80 percent of the company's revenue. While it was essentially a template document, it was obviously a very important one, and quite complex too. As Head of Legal, after a new business partner had signed the document, I would go through it to check that all the essentials were fully and correctly captured, and that it was fully and correctly executed by the business partner, before endorsing that document with my signature. Only then would the relevant executive manager execute the contract on behalf of the company. This was an extremely time-consuming and largely mundane exercise. It was certainly one that I was desperate to rid myself of at the soonest opportunity in order to free up valuable time to focus on deeper work.

So, when this graduate trainee arrived, one of my primary objectives was to hand over this duty to him. I spent a fair amount of time taking him through the document, highlighting and explaining the sections that would need to be adjusted and tailored according to the individual business partner who we were dealing with, and emphasising the gravity of certain aspects and the need for their accuracy. After a few months of overseeing his work in this area, I was confident in the graduate trainee's ability to effectively dis-charge this duty. I duly delegated the task, including the endorsement of the contract, to him and I breathed a sigh of relief. The task was still being done effectively by a person who now understood not only the practical business implications, but also the legalities by virtue of his qualifications. I now had numerous extra hours in my week. This is working smart!

But guess what ...? The executive who would ultimately execute this was having none of it! He insisted that the review and endorsement had to be done by me specifically, and not by the more junior lawyer. This was non-negotiable. I had tried to be innovative. I had assessed the competency level of my subordinate, and made a decision to empower him. I had tried to delegate a time-consuming and mundane task, satisfying myself that the output was not compromised. I had tried to work smart. Ultimately, I failed on all counts because the mindset of the business leadership, and the culture it engendered, would not allow my initiatives to succeed.

But when it comes to working smart, there is one pitfall that trumps all others. It is the archaic notion, which is still surprisingly prevalent, that the people who put in the longest hours are not only the hardest workers, but also the *best* workers. And that this is how everyone should be! So, you find business leaders preaching the *en vogue* "work smart" and "innovation" gospels, yet their mindset – the mindset that sets the corporate culture and, in turn, defines the way people do things on a day-to-day basis – is still strangely fixated on people putting in the long hours, regardless of what they actually produce. Despite what is routinely preached, the culture often favours hard workers over smart workers. And this is another reason flexitime, which we looked at in Chapter 8, doesn't work in many organisations.

Deviating slightly, it is worth pointing out that there also appears to be little consideration for the way the world has changed from decades ago when, indeed, those who stayed at the office late were almost certainly doing it for the benefit of the organisation. In this day and age, it is far more likely that people staying after hours are surfing the net for personal enjoyment or, worse, looking for a new job using the company's internet. The fact that a person is still in the office after hours does not necessarily mean that he is a hard worker. Far from it!

This brings to mind a blog I was reading shortly before I set about writing the book, and a particular portion that stood out for me to the extent that I made a written note of it. Tackling the topic of "working smart", the blogger was very candid in his view that "there is no inherent glory in being the first one in the office and the last one out if you're wasting your time in between. It's better to be the person arriving at noon and leaving at five if you can make those hours more productive". I loved it the moment I read it! Unfortunately, I have failed to find the URL link for reference purposes. Nevertheless, it perfectly sums up the way things should be. But the biggest problem, as with many facets of the corporate world, is that we all know that it is highly theoretical and cannot be implemented unless and until the organisational culture not only allows, but also encourages it.

Where the culture normalises and even glorifies the notion of working long hours, it contradicts any message that may be spoken about working smart, and stifles any attempts to actually work smarter.

CHAPTER 12

BUSINESS PROCESSES

"Optimum business efficiencies" is a term so often thrown about, yet it continues to be something of a mythical creature, as discussed in Chapter 10, that businesses incessantly pursue with very limited success. This is quite simply because, despite this continuous quest, the normal way of doing things – the organisational culture – is characterised by urgency; disregard for and abuse of the most precious of resources – time; and disrespect for the people whose time is being abused. So, where and how do business processes fit into this continuous quest for business efficiencies? Because the primary purpose of formal business processes must, surely, be to optimise business efficiencies, right? We'll come back to this question.

Before going any further, I should take this opportunity to share a maxim we have in the legal profession: "Justice must not only be done, it must also be seen to be done." In a nutshell, this means that where a court of law hands down a judgment, it is not good enough for the judgment to be legally sound. It must be seen, by the lay person, to have given a fair and just outcome. I believe the converse to be true in business:

> *Processes and procedures must not only be seen to exist, they must also actually exist.*

What do I mean by this? I mean that there is a syndrome I have come to notice in business. A syndrome where formal business processes and procedures *do* physically exist – often numerous and very lengthy ones. But, notwithstanding their physical existence, many of them are not well known (or known at all) to the majority. A more accurate and realistic portrayal, therefore, is that these business processes are only *seen to exist* because pieces of paper marked "xyz business process" have, indeed, been crafted and neatly filed away, but – for all intents and purposes – they do not *actually exist*. How can they if they are barely known by those who need to know them and use them, and they are not applied uniformly, consistently or at all? This is one of the things that gives rise to the infamous silo effect that is all too common in business.

This brings me back to the primary purpose of these formal business processes. Once again, it is critical to establish the reason behind your actions, by asking the king of questions – *why*. Why do these processes exist? Why did people spend significant amounts of time and energy crafting and formalising them? The assumption, to repeat, is that they exist to optimise business efficiencies through their proper utilisation and application.

The unfortunate reality in many businesses, however, is that business processes exist primarily to impress certain stakeholders. And, quite ironically, it is those stakeholders who have no involvement in the operations of the business and the use of those business processes, such as shareholders and regulators. Processes are put in place so that when these stakeholders come around and ask about business processes and procedures, a nice file can be presented at the click of a finger, and everyone gets a pat on the back because they are *seen to be* so organised and efficient. As long as this remains the primary purpose behind these business processes, this syndrome will go unabated. Business processes will continue to *be seen to exist*, but will not *actually exist*. And inefficiencies will continue to be the order of the day!

Let's move on, and assume we arrive at the point where the primary purpose behind business processes is rectified. In order for processes to *actually* exist rather than just *be seen* to exist, the culture of urgency and adhocracy must be addressed. As we have discussed, the moment anything becomes classified as urgent, it necessarily means that something has gone wrong and the normal process (whether formally documented or not) can no longer be followed. And while urgent matters are, indeed, unavoidable in business from time to time, when urgency becomes the norm rather than the exception, it necessarily means that deviation from the established business processes also becomes the norm rather than the exception. And so, where there is a culture of urgency, it actually supports, complements and perpetuates this syndrome I keep referring to – where the business is primarily concerned with *being seen to have* the right processes rather than *actually having and following* the right processes.

The formulation of business processes, as I understand things, requires an appreciation of all the inputs required. From that understanding, one can then devise the most efficient way of doing things. The way that is most efficient in the grander scheme of the organisation as a whole. What this means is that the process – *any* process – will almost inevitably be more cumbersome for some individuals than it is for others. But that is the price to be paid for the greater good of the organisation. For overall increased efficiency. Everyone needs to understand this principle and to be on board with it. Everyone needs to appreciate that his task or input is but one in a long chain, and it needs to be done in a certain way and at a certain time so that the next person can pick up and progress rather than having to waste time and energy tidying up or even redoing what has not been done properly by the last person. This requires a good understanding of the bigger picture. To repeat the message from

Chapter 5 and, indeed, the overriding theme of *Life Demystified*, understanding is absolutely critical to the achievement of any goal. This cannot be overstated!

Without this understanding, there will always be a tendency for people to consciously and wilfully disregard established business processes if these processes do not represent the easiest method for them individually. This is simply human nature. It is only with a sound understanding of individual tasks in the context of the bigger picture and the overall desired business output that this tendency will be addressed. Only when there is understanding, will everyone see the real value of following the business processes.

You see, if everyone is clear on why something must be done in a particular way, or at a particular time, or why it must be done at all, then they will do it correctly. But if people only *know* what they are supposed to do without *understanding* the rest, including how it feeds into the tasks of the next person in the next department, tasks will just be performed in any old way, and established business processes will be ineffective.

Make sure business processes exist for the right reason. And then ensure that they are not only known, but also understood.

CHAPTER 13

WHEN MANAGERS DON'T MANAGE

Management is more than just a title!

Experience has shown me that this is a phenomenon that is rife in the business world. Managers, far too often, simply do not manage! But how could this be? This chapter not only explains and demonstrates how this business phenomenon routinely manifests itself but, critically, also explores the reasons behind it.

Personally, I had no exposure to business-related subjects in high school. I chose science subjects at A-Level because I enjoyed them, I was good at them, and my intention at the time was to become a medical doctor. Things took a radical turn, and I landed up in Law School instead, which is a different story for a different day. The closest one comes to business appreciation in Law School is through the Business Law module which is, unsurprisingly, very heavily weighted in favour of the *Law* aspect rather than the *Business* aspect.

I then spent over four years in private practice, honing my skills as a young attorney. Similarly, the closest I got to any form of business appreciation was dealing with the legal problems encountered by my corporate clients. Accordingly, then, my focus was on finding a *legal* solution rather than a *business* solution.

So, when I eventually ventured into the business world as In-house Legal Counsel, it was a completely new world. I found it fascinating then and, well over a decade later, I still do. I have worked for a number of companies of varying size and structure, but I have effectively always held a management role – whether in an official or *de facto* capacity. But, notwithstanding these management roles that I held, it took me many years to come to the realisation that, while I was competent and accomplished from a legal perspective, it was quite the opposite from a management perspective. I guess the most important thing here is that I *did* eventually come to this realisation. Many managers never do!

I knew very little about management and what it means to actually *be* a manager as opposed to just *be called* a manager. With this realisation, I put myself through a couple of management-development courses and I read a few books on the subject. If the shift from legal practice to the business sector was like a new world, then these courses and books opened up my eyes to something of a new universe – that of management in its truest and purest form. It was then that I came to the realisation that far too many "managers" (including myself at one point), actually don't manage. I found myself compelled to analyse this enigma, and in doing so, I eventually came up with two major reasons for it.

The first is pretty obvious. Too many "managers" simply do not have any real appreciation of what it is to manage in the first place. If you don't know what it is to manage, you cannot manage. Simple. Like I said, I used to be one of these people. I believe that a common way in which this situation arises is the practice we see whereby a person is rewarded for technical competence and loyal service. On the face of things, being recognised and rewarded is undoubtedly a good practice. It becomes a problem, however, when this reward takes the form of a promotion which brings with it the coveted title, "Manager", yet the proud new holder of that title doesn't really know what it means to actually *be* a manager as opposed to just *be called* a manager. And, worse, there seems to be no deliberate attempt by employers to address this gap. While this is, to an extent, demonstrative of a certain culture, I think it is far more reflective of a gap that has, perhaps, not been identified by business leaders. To reiterate, there is certainly nothing wrong with this culture of reward through promotion. It just needs some refinement, particularly the additional element of ensuring that the promoted person receives the necessary training to capacitate him to be an effective manager. It's that simple. But as with any gap, it can never be closed if the relevant people have not realised that the gap exists in the first place.

The second reason is much more demonstrative of the prevailing corporate culture. It is the inherent and very apparent reluctance on the part of many senior managers to let go of the reins and let middle and lower managers actually manage, starting with setting of daily, weekly, and monthly plans for their departments and sections, and then allowing those plans to be implemented in the way these managers deem best.

This second reason begins to shed more light on the common go-to response used by senior management which we looked at in Chapter 4 – the cringeworthy "It's strategic!" An educated guess tells me that this response could well be founded upon the same aspect of corporate culture – where senior management simply refuses to let go of the reins. You see, the more information that is shared with middle management and below, the more these people are equipped and empowered to make decisions for themselves and their departments. This, in turn, has the effect of eliminating the need to keep referring decisions – often routine decisions – upwards. So, this most undesirable of responses – "It's strategic!" – could well be very strategic itself, as it presents senior management with a mechanism and an ostensibly good reason to keep information to themselves. And, in so doing, to retain control over all decisions and to preserve the feeling of importance. All this, unfortunately, is at the expense of managers doing what they are supposed to do and at the expense of general business efficiencies. Decision-making is a critical element of effective management, and we'll look at this more a little later.

As I mentioned in Chapter 11, at one point I found myself training and mentoring a law graduate. One of the first things I did was to give him a business-management textbook to read, so that he would not travel the same path that I did – completely oblivious to principles of management. I highlighted to him that if he had any intentions of staying in the corporate sector, he needed to have a good appreciation of business management. Legal competence alone would not suffice. A couple of months later, we discussed what he had picked up from the book, and we went through the functions of management that any management 101 book will invariably unpack. He began by expressing his relief upon reading about the value and necessity of planning. He went on to explain how he would often find himself spending significant chunks of time planning certain tasks but, as he did so, he would always anticipate, very nervously, a situation where he would be asked to account for his time. And he would then panic about how he could come up with an answer that would be deemed acceptable. The conundrum he faced – to his mind anyway – was that while he knew he had spent a considerable amount of time planning, this would not be an acceptable answer because there would be nothing tangible to show for it. In other words, he had not *done* anything (yet), and he assumed this would immediately be frowned upon.

I quickly allayed those fears and encouraged him to carry on with this good practice of planning. But this highlighted something bigger. You see, not only is there a tendency for senior management to disregard the planning process that goes on below them, together with its value, but there is also an apparent and unfortunate acknowledgement and acceptance of this default position at lower levels. So, you begin to see a certain mindset that is shared by all – from executive management to every level below. This is a mindset that is prevalent not because of, but despite, what is formally recorded in managers' job descriptions and other documentation. This is a common mindset that becomes the unwritten rule. And, as we know, it is these unwritten rules that shape and define the organisational culture. Before you know it, you have a culture that serves only to restrict effective management. Or management at all! Planning, to emphasise, is the first function of management, yet it is somehow criminally underrated and undervalued.

Let's get back to decision-making, which

is another critical aspect of management. Yet, again, one routinely finds middle managers afraid to make decisions and instead, referring relatively simple matters to senior management. And, perhaps worse, it is not uncommon to find senior management doing the same and referring relatively routine matters to board and shareholder level for decisions. Decisions that the board and shareholders should really not be burdened with.

In my experience, there are generally few, if any, written rules that say that this should be done. In fact, it is quite the opposite. Many companies have documented values which often include something about "employee empowerment" which, on the face of things, must necessarily include the empowerment to make decisions. Yet the unwritten rules – the rules that define the organisational culture – say something quite different. Perhaps it is the board that has directed senior management to refer all routine decisions upwards and, in so doing, sets the tone for the same practice to be cascaded downwards from senior management to middle management and so on. And so, you find a culture where decision-making becomes a privilege enjoyed by the select few rather than a normal function of management. And this is coupled with a culture of fear. Executive management is afraid to make decisions without referring them to the board, and that fear cascades all the way down.

Managers need to know what it is to actually

manage and, with this knowledge, they must then be genuinely empowered to do so! For managers to effectively manage, the culture has to allow it. Without a conducive culture, the good managers will spend their time trying to control their frustrations instead of doing what they are supposed to be doing – managing!

Without a culture that allows and genuinely supports effective management, managers are reduced to glorified doers of ad hoc tasks.

PART V
PEOPLE

CHAPTER 14

"WE VALUE OUR PEOPLE."

Valued staff = Happy staff;
Happy staff = Happy customers

We've all heard this "we value our people" song before. Perhaps once too often. Business leaders keep singing it, perhaps in the hope that the words alone will, almost magically, make staff feel valued despite the daily actions that contradict these overused words. As I opined in Part I, whatever happens and doesn't happen in an organisation is down to the corporate culture. And the corporate culture is *not* what the leaders of that organisation say it is. Rather, it is what the ordinary people within the organisation say it is, based on their daily dealings with each other. If staff are genuinely valued, it is because the culture is that way inclined rather than because they are continually told as much. And, perhaps most interestingly, if staff genuinely feel valued because of the way they are treated on a daily basis, they will not need to be expressly told that they are valued.

There is a now-famous quote by Sir Richard Branson: "Clients do not come first. Employees come first. If you take care of your employees, they will take care of the clients." This makes perfect sense. Regardless of the customer-service policies and charters that may be in place, your staff interact with your customers. If your staff are frustrated and disengaged, this mood will inevitably filter through in their dealings with customers, whether you like it or not. And by the same token, if your staff feel valued, they will be happy and engaged. This, too, will filter through in their dealings with customers.

As we've touched on, many companies have carefully crafted sets of values, and these very often include something about the way employees are valued. I have seen some that go as far as saying that the people are their *most important* resource. And these values are proudly and brashly brandished on company profiles and websites for the world to see.

I worked for one such company, and I remember how taken aback I was when, in a strategic planning session, one of the executives openly and matter-of-factly declared that these values serve primarily as a marketing tool, and should not be taken too literally. With each head of department having effectively been told that the values that the company has claimed to live by thus far were a marketing gimmick, the expressions around the room were priceless!

So, notwithstanding what is routinely preached and what may be stated in the official values of the organisation, the real question is, or at least ought to be, "Do our people feel like they are valued?" despite the farce that the official values are reduced to in many organisations. Or, put another way: "Does the organisational culture promote a genuine feeling, on the part of the employees, that they are valued?" Getting an accurate answer to these questions entails much more than simply asking the people, "Do you feel valued?" Employee-engagement surveys are a common feature of many businesses, but they have their obvious shortcomings, which we look at more in Chapter 17. Surveys may bring us closer to answering the important questions, but not close enough.

The truth is that business leaders should have a fairly good inherent understanding of the *real* value they attach to their people – marketing gimmicks aside. And this should be based on the way they, as business leaders, treat their people on a day-to-day basis. If they do not already have this understanding, they can easily get it by carrying out a simple self-introspection and quick analysis of their general behaviour and attitude towards employees; the expectations they place on employees; and, in a nutshell and most importantly, whether they actually see them as *people* or just *employees* that are one of many resources that the business makes use of. This is a critical distinction!

Everybody knows that businesses exist to make money. Shareholders invest their money and expect a return. They appoint a competent board of directors to steer the business in the right direction. From there, strategies and associated actions cascade down to all levels of employees to contribute towards their implementation and, in a nutshell, to make as much money as possible for the shareholders. It is the employees, down to the very lowest level, who must work tirelessly to make the business profitable. But at what cost?

Let's get back to this critical distinction I mentioned. If employees are genuinely valued, there will be a constant and deliberate acknowledgement and appreciation, first and foremost, that these are people and not machines or "just another resource" that the business makes use of; and, second, that being an employee of this organisation is merely one of the many aspects of every person's life. They have lives outside the workplace. They have things that are important to them outside the workplace.

> *The main reason and in some cases the only reason that employees get up and go to work every day is to make the other facets of their lives – the facets outside the workplace – better!*

So, when the demands of the job significantly compromise and adversely affect the quality of life outside the job, what is really going on? Where's the sense in it all? Is this person really valued? Is this person even viewed as a person at all, or as just another replaceable resource along with production plants, machinery and everything else the business uses for the sole purpose of making as much money as possible for the shareholders?

It is common for businesses to have huge capex (capital-expenditure) budgets, and they then utilise these budgets on things like expensive pieces of machinery, again, with the sole purpose of maximising profits. And it will be instilled in everyone concerned that this is a very expensive piece of machinery and should be treated accordingly. If the operating manual says it must be used for a maximum of eight hours per day, you can bet your bottom dollar that everyone will know this and will religiously adhere to it, *without* the business leaders having to keep preaching about how they value their machinery. Yet, conversely, many businesses will not only allow, but also expect and insist that their people work well in excess of eight hours per day, despite the very prominent message – internally and externally – about how employees are valued. Depending on the level of the employee, there will often be no overtime compensation for this either. There is no second thought given to the physical and mental strain routinely placed on people. So, realistically and objectively speaking, what is valued more by the business and its leaders under such circumstances – the machinery or the people? And under such circumstances, can the people be expected to genuinely feel valued at all?

This is a common aspect of corporate culture I have come to notice. One where business leaders will squeeze everything they can out of their people, and think nothing of it. It is so rife that I believe it warrants a separate book altogether, which I shall certainly begin working on in the near future. It is, essentially, the routine brainwashing of employees into giving *everything* to the business, at the expense of every other aspect of their lives. I think one appropriate title for this book would be *Brainwashed!* because rather than *valued*, this is really what many employees are.

If a person is genuinely valued, there will be a conscious effort to understand what is important to that person outside the workplace and, with that understanding, a deliberate effort to allow that person to attend to those things that are important to him. It might be that the person wants to get home in time to see their new baby before bedtime. It might be that the person has been working towards running a marathon and needs time after work to train. It may be that a person is working on a personal project after hours, with a view to launching his own business in the future. It may even be something so basic as a person going on a family vacation for a week and simply hoping not to be bombarded with calls and emails from the office, or not being expected to check emails in the first place. Whatever an employee is doing in his personal life, work–life balance must not only be respected, but must also be promoted if employees are genuinely valued. As long as the leadership is focused only on maximising profits and has no interest in what is important to their people outside the workplace, there is no way they can genuinely claim to place any real value on those people. This can only be changed through cultural transformation.

Some business leaders actually like to make a point of asking their people the toxic question, "How are you adding value?" Immediately, the person on the receiving end of this question is up against the ropes, and this is discussed in detail in the next chapter. Whether intended or not, this question automatically becomes rhetorical, and is quickly reduced from a question to a very thinly-veiled statement: "I do not believe you are adding value." And, strangely, this goes on against the backdrop of constant preaching of how the people are valued.

These are just a few examples of what really goes on in many organisations. While business leaders continue to preach, *ad nauseum*, about how they value their people, it is far more important to reflect on whether the day-to-day practices and routines are likely or unlikely to make any normal person feel genuinely valued. This is common sense, and it should be reflected in the corporate culture. A classic example of the old adage, "Actions speak louder than words"!

If people are to be genuinely valued, first recognise them as people rather than just employees. Second, acknowledge that as people, there are more important things in their lives than this job. Third, allow them the time to spend on those more important things!

CHAPTER 15

"HOW ARE YOU ADDING VALUE?"

"Value addition" appears to have become another one of these trendy, *en vogue* catchphrases in the corporate world over the past couple of years. In my experience, many business leaders seem to feel compelled to keep bandying it about amongst their subordinates, more because it has become the done thing rather, most ironically, than because of the value that this catchphrase adds. And then, there are the unfortunate employees who not only have to put up with the overuse and abuse of this term, but also find themselves on the receiving end of the dreaded question, "How are you adding value?"

"Value addition" or "adding value" can be expanded, according to my understanding, to "adding *shareholder* value". In a nutshell, the shareholders are looking for maximum financial return on what they have invested in this business. Against this backdrop, it is imperative to adopt an inclusive view of the business as a whole, and how each person and each department performs different but equally important functions, all aimed at achieving one common, final goal. There are obviously the departments or divisions that generate income, and perhaps their value speaks for itself through the top line. But what about the support functions? It is the people in these departments who commonly fall victim to this dreaded value-addition question, specifically because they do not generate income. This is despite their tireless work behind the scenes to ensure that they are reducing and eliminating huge hidden costs that come with all sorts of potential liabilities, reputational damage and other problems, over and above the costs of having to outsource the services that are now being provided internally. While they do not impact the top line, their efforts in reducing and eliminating these costs obviously impact the overall objective, which is the bottom line – the profitability. And positively so! If the support functions are actively and positively contributing to the one common, final goal, is this not adding value? By virtue of their very existence, these departments and the people in them *must be* adding value. If they are not, then the departments would surely not exist in the first place.

Now, if you happen to be the person who finds yourself being asked how you are adding value to the business, the immediate and obvious implication is that you are *not* adding value. Fully aware of this implication – as any employee of average intelligence would be – you may, firstly, be wondering what exactly is meant by "adding value". Surprising as it may sound, many people don't have a good understanding of this term, and its mention serves only to cause panic and confusion. In some cases, that is the precisely the intention! This is exacerbated by the fact that many business leaders, in my opinion anyway, tend to use this term out of context. But, of course, you dare not ask because this would be construed as an admission of guilt. For how could you possibly be adding value if you don't even know what it means to be adding value in the first place? So, the inevitable outcome is that you begin rambling on, reciting a plethora of the good things – whether relevant or not – that you do, all in a bid to convince your boss that you are, in fact, "adding value". Before going any further, I should share what I believe to be the first of two rules of thumb when it comes to "adding value":

The default position must be that any and every role in any organisation must necessarily be adding value by virtue merely of its existence.

Every role exists because a conscious decision has been made, at some point, that this particular role is necessary for the business to operate at an optimal level. But this default position has to stem from a culture of genuine value attached to people, which we looked at in detail in the previous chapter. And this highlights another reason for the confusion and panic that sets in when this dreaded value-addition question arises. You see, the average person diligently performs his daily duties and, almost subconsciously, believes that this default position does, in fact, exist. This default position that, in diligently performing his duties, he is obviously adding value. Otherwise, why is he being paid to perform those duties every day? So when, all of a sudden, he is asked, "How are you adding value?" the confusion and panic are understandable, if not expected.

From my experience, I have identified four main scenarios in which this question of value addition could possibly come up, and we shall look at each one individually.

The first arises from a situation where there has been some significant change in the business which renders a particular role within that business no longer necessary. Common examples would be a drastic shift in business model or technological advancement. In such instances, the question of value addition has nothing to do with the person filling the role but rather the very existence of the role. In such instances, the solution is simply to phase out that particular role altogether and deal with the person in terms of established employment laws. The solution is *not* to ask questions like, "How are you adding value?"

The second situation is one of incompetence

or, far more common, sub-standard performance. In other words, the role is necessary and unquestionably adds value, which is why it exists. But the person filling that role is not meeting expectations and, therefore, perhaps not adding enough value or any value at all. The issue is not one of value addition but rather one of competence or performance, with the latter being uncompromisingly tied to cultural entropy and employee engagement. It should, therefore, be addressed as such through training or, if necessary, disciplinary proceedings and possible dismissal. Again, it should *not* be dealt with by asking questions like, "How are you adding value?"

The third scenario fits somewhere between the first two aforementioned. It arises where a person is filling a particular role as defined by a job description, yet there is a feeling that, somehow, there should be more coming from this person and this role. I have found this situation to be very common. Once again, this is not an issue with the person. The issue is that the job description needs to be relooked at. The incumbent is doing what the job description dictates and what he thinks is expected of him. There is clearly an expectation gap. If that person is deemed not to be adding enough value or any value at all, then the obvious solution is to revise, refine or redefine the role so that whoever is filling it is adding the desired value. The expectation gap must be closed. The solution, yet again, is *not* to ask questions like, "How are you adding value?"

The second and third scenarios above present an opportune moment to share my second rule of thumb when it comes to "adding value". And it is actually very simple:

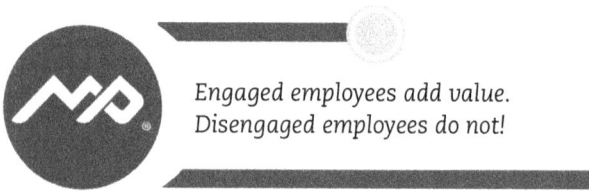

Engaged employees add value.
Disengaged employees do not!

Let's unpack this rule of thumb. When there is sub-standard performance and an employee is not meeting expectations, it could be for any number of reasons. But every one of those reasons can, and certainly should, be traced back to employee engagement – whether directly or indirectly. Similarly, even when a person is meeting the requirements of a job description but, as canvassed in the third scenario above, there is a feeling that there should be more coming from this person and this role, it is directly linked to employee engagement. You see, an engaged employee will always go beyond expectation, and they will do so because they want to. We deal with employee engagement in much more detail in Chapter 17.

The fourth scenario is by far the worst, and there is an element of it in all of the other three. It is when there is a hidden agenda with no objective basis. And no matter what facts are presented, they are not deemed acceptable. I'll give an example of a personal experience. In one of my previous jobs, I was on the receiving end of this very question from my CEO. Perhaps to his surprise, I was not struck with panic and confusion. Instead, I presented objective facts and figures. I am a lawyer by profession, and the value of legal professionals' time is set by an independent authority – the Law Society. And it is based on one's level of experience. The value of my time at that point was US$210 per hour according the prevailing Law Society of Zimbabwe tariffs. I should perhaps repeat and emphasise, this was the objective value of my time set by a regulating authority, not by me. Doing the simple arithmetic, US$210 per hour x eight hours per day x 22 working days per month x 12 months = US$443 520 per annum. Simple and objective. The company was, of course, paying a very small fraction of that in the form of my remuneration, and in return was getting something of significantly higher value. This was before getting to risks and liabilities I had mitigated and avoided by virtue of fulfilling my role. Despite the fact that the company was benefitting from services worth close to half a million dollars each year, my CEO shot down my facts and figures, saying that this was not what he was talking about. Yet, funny enough, he was at a loss to explain properly, or at all, what he *was* talking about and what he *did* mean by this *en vogue* term, "value addition". I immediately saw that there was some hidden agenda there.

In pretty much every aspect of life, it is easy to point out what you *don't* want. But unless and until you can and do point out exactly what it is that you *do* want, there is only one person to blame when you don't get it. If there is no clear expectation on "adding value", then the person who has not clarified his/her expectation is the one at fault, not the person who is suddenly being accused of failing to meet an expectation of which they were never aware. This is surely common sense!

I like to take principles from the legal profession and apply them to various other aspects of life. As far as the law is concerned, every person is presumed innocent until proven guilty. We all know this. But in the corporate world, this toxic question – "How are you adding value?" – has the effect of inverting this established legal principle such that the person on the receiving end is immediately presumed to be guilty of not adding value. And, worse, judgement has probably already been passed before the question is asked. There is no objective and impartial process by which someone can "prove their innocence".

No person in the workplace should ever be asked, "How are you adding value?"! In short, it is a question pregnant with toxicity, and it betrays an equally toxic culture. A corporate culture where there is inherent derision rather than value for people.

It is imperative to distinguish between a role, and the person filling that role. And the default position should always be that every person is adding value by competently filling a role that has been deemed necessary for the business to operate optimally.

CHAPTER 16

TEAMWORK OR PICKING UP SOMEONE'S SLACK?

"Some animals are more equal than others."

This is a syndrome that forms one of the central themes of George Orwell's *Animal Farm*. I have come to notice that this very syndrome is highly prevalent in the corporate world, and it often manifests itself through another term that is overused, misused and abused – "teamwork". This is an ostensibly positive term, but behind this veil of positivity lies a highly manipulative weapon that is often used to coerce certain people into performing tasks that they really should not be doing. So, let us look at what "teamwork" really means or what it should mean in an organisation.

The term is obviously taken from the sporting

world, which provides the best place to start our analysis. For me, there is no better demonstration of teamwork than the 4 x 100m relay. Here you have four individuals, each tasked with running one leg – a quarter – of the race. Each individual must do so to the best of his ability and then, after doing his part fully, he passes the baton on to the next team member. The next team member must receive that baton, and then do the same. It should be emphasised that each team member *must* finish his leg of the race *before* passing the baton on. If one person – one team member – fails to complete his leg well, or at all, the whole team fails in its common goal, which is to finish (and win) the race as a whole. There is no prize for the team member who runs his leg in record time if the others do not do their part.

You will never see one member of a relay team running half of his leg and then attempting to pass on the baton at that stage. Similarly, if one team member drops the baton, his teammates cannot pick it up for him. He must go back, pick it up himself, and then do whatever he needs to do in order to get to the end of his leg and, only then, pass on the baton. Going further, you will never see a team member refusing to accept the baton being passed to him, and instead expecting his team member to carry on running a second leg.

In the corporate world, there will inevitably be a number of business processes, each requiring different inputs from different individuals across different departments. We covered this in detail in Part IV. These individual inputs are all aimed at reaching one final result for the business – one overall team goal! Aside from and despite the syndrome where business processes are *seen to exist* rather than *actually existing*, I firmly believe that every person must surely be aware of the general principle that when they perform a piece of work and pass it on to the next person in the next department, there is an expectation that the work has been done properly and completely so that the next person can progress rather than having to come back because the work hasn't been done properly. Yet in the corporate world – quite the opposite of a relay race – it is almost the norm to find certain individuals *not* completing their leg of the race and attempting to pass on the baton prematurely. They expect the person receiving the baton to first tidy up the existing mess, and then to go on to complete the next leg as well. Alternatively, you find individuals simply not taking up the baton when they are supposed to, and happily watching someone else running the next leg of the race for them.

How often do you find half-baked reports or incomplete information being passed on, with the receiving person having little option but to tidy it up or fill in the gaps if the overall task is to have any hope of completion? Several times I have sat in credit meetings as Head of the Legal Department in various organisations. And several times, my colleagues have piped up in the meeting, much to my surprise, "It has been handed over to Legal." To use another sports analogy, this is a vicious curveball, yet we are supposed to be on the same team! Technically, this comment would be true. But if you dig a little deeper, you will find that this "handing over to Legal" took the form of a two-line email which was sent five minutes before the credit meeting, saying, "This debt is over 90 days and we have not made any progress with the debtor. It should now be recovered through legal channels." There is not one single piece of information or documentation attached, so there is really nothing that can be done by the Legal Department. There is no baton for the Legal Department to carry forward towards the common finish line. But the meeting minutes will show that the debt is now sitting with Legal, so someone has succeeded in getting this monkey off their back. Whether or not the next leg of the race can be run seems to be of no concern. And when the Legal personnel have made little, if any, progress by the time the next credit meeting comes around, questions will naturally be asked of them. Yet, quite curiously, questions are not asked about how this matter was "handed over" in the first place and why there is no information that allows the Legal Department to take it up and run the next leg.

Of course, there are situations in business where the person who is supposed to perform a certain task becomes incapacitated and genuinely needs help completing his leg. But, just like the issue of urgency, these instances should be the exception rather than the rule. And in such instances, there should be clear and express communication acknowledging that the first leg has not been completed and asking for help to complete it.

Let's get back to the *Animal Farm* culture, where some animals are more equal than others. For readers who may not be familiar with Animal Farm, let me give a brief overview before going any further. The animals on one Manor Farm take a stance and rebel against the farmer with the intention of replacing the oppressive conditions they had been subjected to with a free and equal society. They take over the farm and immediately come up with a number of commandments by which they will now live, the most important being "All animals are equal". And indeed, in the early days following the rebellion, all animals are seen and treated as equals. But the general state of affairs on the farm begins to decay as certain animals see fit to attach more importance to themselves. Eventually, the founding commandments are cast aside altogether and replaced by one solitary commandment:- "All animals are equal, but some animals are more equal than others".

In line with observations made in the previous chapter, the general trend I have noticed – from my own experiences and from several discussions I have had with fellow corporate professionals – seems to be that those who directly generate income are more equal and those in the support functions are less equal. I once sat in a strategic planning session where one of the executives expressly confirmed this, much to the amazement of everyone present. You could cut the tension with a knife, not only in that meeting, but also around the office for several weeks after.

With this *Animal Farm* culture, it is very easy for the more equal animals to pass on the responsibility for their work to less-equal personnel in other departments. They are in a position whereby they can purport to have passed on the baton without having properly completed their leg of the race. The less equal animal simply has to suck it up, and effectively complete two legs of the race. Alternatively (or in addition), you find the more equal animal simply refusing to take up the baton from less equal colleagues after the previous leg has been run. And the story will be that the person who has completed his leg and has tried (and failed) to hand over the baton, is the one holding things up. You see, the less equal animal – by virtue of being less equal – is in no position to highlight that he doesn't have enough information to work with to complete his leg of the race; or that he has, in fact, completed his leg of the race and is waiting for the next person to take up the baton. If he tries to raise these concerns, he will simply be labelled as someone who is not being a team player. His teamwork will be said to be poor.

This syndrome of passing on the baton before

one completes his leg of the race becomes the norm because the organisational culture allows the people who do it to hide behind "teamwork". It is the organisational culture that (wrongly) defines "teamwork" to include picking up someone else's slack. It is the organisational culture that does not enforce accountability for one's own actions and/ or omissions. It is an organisational culture of fear, where certain people – the less equal animals – feel like there is no option but to pick up someone else's slack in the name of "teamwork". Ironically, this is actually an organisational culture that is masquerading as one that values teamwork but, in reality, is quite the opposite. You have people handing things over for the primary purpose of just getting it off their desk rather than to give the next person something they can actually work with towards the common team goal. It is an organisational culture that condones laziness and/ or incompetence because, save for the odd genuine exception, these are the real reasons for people routinely not completing tasks properly.

This brings back memories of Law School and, in particular, one of my professors. I won't name him, but I hope he reads this book one day. And if he does, he will certainly know that it's him being referred to. We were speaking about assignments, and he made a point of mentioning how he hates the idea of group assignments. It is a fact of life – so he told us – that in any group activity, there will be those who do more than their fair share of work to compensate for the others. To compensate for "the slackers"! As young adults, still very naïve in the art of life, we all found this quite amusing, as much because of the terminology than anything. But despite this comical choice of vocabulary, the message was most apt. The question that needs to be asked by business leaders is whether the prevailing culture encourages slackers and allows them to hide behind "teamwork".

My conclusion is simple. Teamwork means each person in the process chain performing his/her task fully and properly, and being in sync with each other towards one team goal. It means facilitating and allowing the next person in the process chain to pick up the task and move forwards, not backwards.

Teamwork is not picking up the slack of lazy or incompetent colleagues who have chosen not to have done their part properly!

CHAPTER 17

EMPLOYEE ENGAGEMENT

Engaged employees are more pro-ductive and more valuable.

Employees keep the wheels of business turning. This is a fact, whether anyone cares to acknowledge it or not. So, if the employees are doing things half-heartedly, the wheels of the business are not turning as they should be. This is common logic. With these observations, it becomes easy to see why employee engagement is, or at least should be, a critical aspect in any business. Perhaps *the* most critical!

You will recall from Part III that I classified "time" as *the most valuable resource any organisation has*. I went on to explain that time does not exist in a vacuum. It exists through, and belongs to, people. But if your people are not engaged, how can you expect them to manage their time well? And how can you expect them to devote their office hours to the full benefit of the organisation rather than while away the working day on social media websites or, worse, on recruitment websites, looking to move on to greener pastures at the first available opportunity? That is when they aren't complaining, to every co-worker who will listen, about everything that is wrong with the organisation. When you look at it this way, it becomes very easy to see how employee engagement is easily the most critical aspect of any business. It directly impacts the way people use their time – the most precious resource – as well as the manner in which they perform every single task. Or whether they perform certain tasks at all!

I have come across many definitions of this term, "employee engagement". And after much consideration, I would say that employee engagement is the overall manifestation of the *unwritten* contract between employer and employee. Of everything that is not expressly stated in the written/formal employment contract but is, nonetheless, expected by an employee.

To expand, employee engagement is a product of the extent to which the employer has met all the unwritten obligations which the employee believes that the employer should meet. Whether or not the employer actually meets these obligations is, in turn, a product of the overall organisational culture. Employee engagement and organisational culture, therefore, are inseparably linked and the former, together with cultural entropy (which we discussed in Chapter 2), is probably the best indicator of the latter. In fact, I have come up with a very simplified equation (assuming the higher the corporate-culture rating, the better the culture is):

Employee engagement minus Cultural entropy = Prevailing corporate culture.

There is a common tendency to confuse employee satisfaction with employee engagement, and to incorrectly use these terms interchangeably. These are two very different concepts! Any number of things could increase employee satisfaction without having any positive impact on their productivity and their value to the organisation. Many employees are highly satisfied if they show up, do as little as possible, and then get paid every month. Employee engagement, on the other hand, directly impacts the employee's productivity and value to the organisation.

Employee engagement tells you the extent to which employees are willing to go beyond expectation for the benefit of the employer. Let me repeat that. Employee engagement tells you the extent that an employee is *willing* to go beyond the call of duty, not for his own benefit, but *for the bene-*

fit of the employer. Two critical elements stand out. "Willing" is the first. Engaged employees go beyond expectation *because they want to*. Because they are totally on board with the overall purpose and they know that they are valued and appreciated. Not because they are forced to do so, and not out of fear. The second is "for the benefit of the employer". Engaged employees go the extra mile, *at the expense of their personal lives*. Similarly, this is because they are totally on board with the overall purpose and they know that they are valued and appreciated.

Despite the fact that employee satisfaction and employee engagement are two very different concepts, there is a strange and somewhat inversely proportional relationship between the two. It is a relationship which is seldom noticed, let alone spoken about. You see, the prevailing conditions or the aspects of the organisational culture that generally lead to increased employee satisfaction for low-performing employees, are the very same conditions or aspects that lead to decreased employee engagement of higher-performing employees. Admittedly, this may sound a bit cryptic at this stage. The simple graph shown in Figure 17.1 on the next page together with some specific and realistic examples should illustrate this concept.

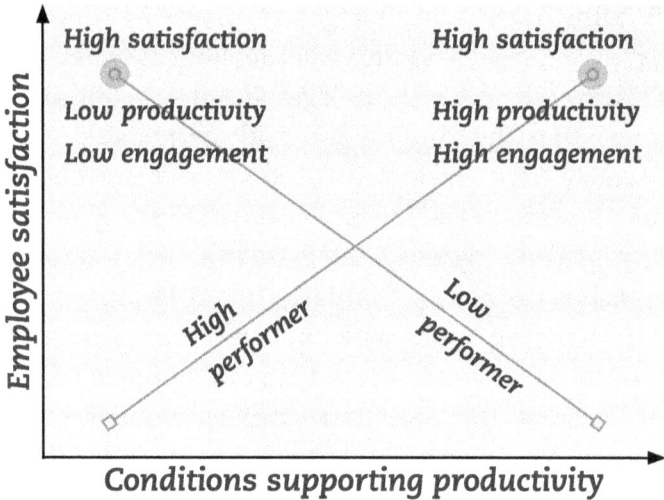

Figure 17.1: Employee satisfaction and employee engagement – a critical comparison

In every organisation, there are those who are poor planners and poor time managers. We all know this, and we probably also know *who* the culprits are in our respective organisations. They leave things to the eleventh hour, and then expect everyone to run around frantically. When the organisational culture allows urgency to become the norm, it effectively means that the poor planner is able to routinely dump his inefficiency on his colleague's desk at the last minute, with a sticky note saying "URGENT". The latter's well-thought-out plans must then, necessarily, be discarded to accommodate and cover for the former's poor planning. As a result, the poor planner is probably pretty satisfied in his job while the good planner becomes frustrated and disengaged.

You may also have an employee who lacks certain skills and competencies that he should really have. But he is able to manipulate the system (and the corporate politics) to routinely get the better and more competent performers to tidy up his mess in the name of "teamwork", which we looked at in the previous chapter. Unsurprisingly, then, you have one person who is very satisfied because he has found a way of keeping his job despite his incompetence; and another person who grows increasingly frustrated and disengaged because he is having to routinely do someone else's job (as well as his own).

To repeat, employee engagement is an aspect, together with cultural entropy, that probably gives the greatest insight into the culture of an organisation. But this presents yet another paradox. In organisations with the best culture, the employees are highly engaged and will answer employee-engagement survey questions openly and honestly. In these organisations, employee-engagement surveys will give accurate results, but they are not really necessary because the high levels of engagement are self-evident. In organisations with a poor culture, on the other hand – where there is a real need to gauge employee engagement through surveys and other means – the employees are far more likely to be fearful of answering survey questions honestly. The employer, therefore, gets inaccurate feedback and the status *quo* – the undesirable culture – is perpetuated.

But here's the thing. While I do believe that employee-engagement surveys and resultant indexes have their value (under the correct conditions, of course), I am firmly of the view that employers *must*, surely, have a fair idea of the engagement levels of employees *without* any such survey having been conducted. This is closely related to the self-introspection I mentioned in Chapter 14 that business leaders should carry out to establish the real value they attach to their people. And, with this knowledge, they either choose to do something about it, or they choose to turn a blind eye. In many cases, when you see an employer deciding to conduct an employee-engagement survey, it is like a parent taking their child for cholesterol tests, knowing very well the junk they feed that child every day, but somehow hoping for a result they know is not possible!

A prerequisite for employee engagement is a decent understanding of human beings and their expectations. I speak about this at length in *Life Demystified*. In a nutshell, there is a need to understand the needs and desires of human beings which, in turn, will shed light on what their expectations are and what motivates them. Maslow's hierarchy of human needs is invaluable, despite certain flaws it has. The main flaw, which I believe everyone should be cognisant of when looking at this valuable blueprint, is the implication that people are motivated in a sequential manner starting from the bottom of the pyramid going up. In other words, people cannot be motivated by higher-tier items until they have all the items on the tiers below.

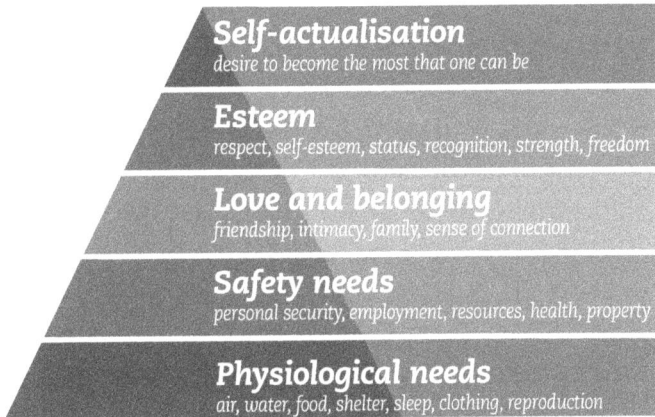

Self-actualisation
desire to become the most that one can be

Esteem
respect, self-esteem, status, recognition, strength, freedom

Love and belonging
friendship, intimacy, family, sense of connection

Safety needs
personal security, employment, resources, health, property

Physiological needs
air, water, food, shelter, sleep, clothing, reproduction

Figure 17.2: Maslow's hierarchy of needs
Source: Maslow, A.H. (1943), "A Theory of Human Motivation", *Psychological Review* 50(4), pp. 370–96

If, as a business leader, you understand your people, you will then have a good idea of what their expectations are. If you have a good idea of what their expectations are, you will be well placed to meet those expectations. It should go without saying that you cannot meet expectations of whose very existence you are not aware. If you are able to, and do, meet the expectations of your people, you have happy, productive and engaged employees, as illustrated in Figure 17.3.

Simple! Or perhaps not?

Employees meet and exceed employer's expectations

↑

Employees become highly engaged

↑

Employer meets employees' expectations

↑

Employer understands employees' expectations

↑

Employer understands employees as people

↑

Culture of understanding
AND
Culture of genuine value attached to people

Figure 17.3: The foundations for engaged employees

This is simple in theory, but less so in reality. And, as always, we must look at things realistically and try to find real solutions to real problems. You see, identifying and meeting the expectations of your staff can never happen as long as the organisational culture doesn't place a focus on people. We spoke about this at length in Chapter 14. If you genuinely value your staff, and you want them to be engaged, they need to be viewed and treated as *people* rather than just *employees*. As people who have lives and corresponding expectations outside the workplace and outside their capacity as employees. Where the default position is for managers to fob off their staff to the Human Resources Department every time there is a concern to be addressed, that is an immediate sign that the organisational culture is not one that is conducive to employee engagement. People management is a critical component of every business leader, manager and supervisor's job. And this *must* be ingrained in the organisational culture.

The unfortunate reality in many organisations is that the *modus operandi* of business leaders is to try and temporarily pacify and, if we are being candid, to fool employees into believing that their concerns are being addressed. And then to wash their hands of the problem and refer these employees to the Human Resources Department which, in reality, has no authority, mandate or power to truly address the concerns. And these are the same business leaders , in conjunction with the

Human Resources Department, who decide that it's a good idea to conduct an employee-engagement survey as if they don't already know that employees are disengaged. An employee-engagement survey under these conditions is, quite simply, a façade! It is consistent with the *modus operandi* which is to fool employees into thinking that there is an interest in their engagement and general well-being. But here's the thing ... the more intelligent employees can read between the lines and see through this façade. They know what is really happening. They are not being fooled! Ironically, the employees whom you succeed in fooling are the ones you can, and probably should, be doing without.

The more intelligent, more driven and more productive employees are not being fooled by corporate politics. They are being further disengaged. Don't treat your people like fools and expect them to be engaged.

PART VI
CONCLUSION

CHAPTER 18

BRINGING IT ALL TOGETHER

Quite simply, the prevailing corporate culture determines everything that happens and doesn't happen in an organisation! Everything!

• What is organisational culture?

The culture of an organisation, or the corporate culture as it is often called, is *not* what its business leaders say it is. And it is *not* based on what may be documented within the organisation. It is what the people within that organisation – all the way down to the lowest level of employee – will say about it if they are given a platform to speak openly and honestly without any cloud of fear hanging over their heads.

Organisational culture is the common set of day-to-day behaviours, beliefs and expectations of all the people within an organisation, regardless of what is formally documented. The corporate culture may well be consistent with what is formally documented. But in equal likelihood, it may not!

This is the starting point and, unfortunately, the point where many business leaders go wrong. They believe that by simply documenting what you want the culture to be, and repeating it *ad nauseum*, that's what the culture will be. Wrong!

• Cultural entropy

Corporate culture must be consistently managed. For anything to be managed, it must be measured. But what is the measure of an intangible thing like corporate culture? A great measure is cultural entropy which, most lamentably, is a concept that is relatively unknown to, let alone measured by, many business leaders.

Cultural entropy tells you the level of dysfunction; the amount of unproductive energy used; the level of friction; and, generally, the extent to which the culture of the organisation negatively affects the people within it.

It is something that every business leader needs to know about, and measure.

• Culture versus strategy: the running battle

Strategic planning sessions are held annually (or more frequently) and these often last for days. Strategic objectives and related plans are discussed, debated and, eventually, set. Everyone goes back to the office, and begins implementation. And this will work perfectly well if, and it's a big *if*, the prevailing culture is consistent with and supports the strategy.

But seldom is the culture of an organisation given the time it deserves, or any time at all, in these sessions. A major gap amongst many business leaders is the failure to recognise the fact that everything that happens and doesn't happen in an organisation is a product of the prevailing culture. Where the culture is not aligned to the strategy, it becomes a running battle – culture versus strategy. But in this battle, there will only ever be one winner.

In the words of Peter Drucker, "Culture eats strategy for breakfast." Every day!

- **"It's strategic!"**
Linked to the prerequisite of aligning the culture and the strategy, is the manner in which issues relating to the business strategy are communicated (or not communicated) to staff. In many organisations, there is an underlying notion that strategy and strategic issues are the preserve of the elite few. And this notion is tacitly confirmed and perpetuated by those elite, primarily because it makes them feel important. And so, you find them giving ridiculous answers like, "It's strategic!" in order to preserve the seemingly indispensable feeling of importance.

How can a strategy be implemented when the people trying to execute it are given this kind of response?

A culture that supports strategy implementation cannot accommodate answers like, "It's strategic!"

• Understanding

Understanding is the most essential element in achieving *anything*, including strategic objectives. Not only must every person in an organisation *know* what they need to do, they also need to *understand* it. They need to be clear on why they need to do those things, how they will do them, when they will do them, and who has an interest in those things that they plan to do. This is what understanding is – the state you arrive at when you know exactly what you are aiming to do, and have absolute clarity of why you are doing it, how you will do it, and when you will do it.

And business leaders need to have a sound understanding of what is happening and what needs to happen around them, otherwise impossible timeframes will be set and irrelevant metrics will be measured.

Goals understood are goals achieved!

• Time: Abused, undervalued and disrespected

Time is the single most valuable and important resource available to any person and to any organisation. I rate it as the single most valuable and important because, unlike any other resource, it can never be replaced. Never!

Yet, somehow, despite this incomparable value and importance it carries, time is criminally wasted, abused and disrespected as a matter of routine. And time is inseparable from people. When you abuse and disrespect a person's time, you disrespect and abuse the person to whom the time belongs.

- ## "It's urgent!"

Part of this routine wastage, abuse and disrespect of time comes in the form of the over-used and dreaded declaration, "It's urgent!" This statement means two things, which are seldom realised. First, something has gone wrong such that there must be a deviation from standard procedure. Second, the person on the receiving end of this dreaded statement must, necessarily, drop everything to attend to this matter because "it's urgent". And in the process, all the time spent planning, which now has to be dropped in the name of urgency, has been wasted!

There is no doubt that urgent matters arise from time to time. It is an unavoidable aspect of business. But when urgency is accepted as the norm rather than the exception, it means that the organisational culture has normalised urgency. And this is a serious problem. It serves only to perpetuate something that is going wrong!

• Flexitime: friend or foe?

Flexitime is a tool that is available to businesses. And just like any tool, if it is used properly, it makes your life easier and it is your friend, but if it is not used properly, it loses its value and it becomes a foe.

Every tool has a purpose. The purpose of flexitime is to reduce the wastage of time, whether it is time wasted on commuting or otherwise. The purpose of flexitime is *not* to provide a mechanism for justifying ridiculous working hours. If this is the intention behind the use of flexitime, then it betrays a culture of abuse of people and their time.

Flexitime is founded upon trust. The people who are supposed to make use of this tool must be trusted to do so properly. But it is not uncommon for questions like, "How do we know that he is putting in the full eight hours a day?" to be asked. If you, as a manager or supervisor at any level, find yourself asking this sort of question, there is clearly a culture of inherent mistrust and flexitime will never work.

• Interruptions: the unseen plague

Contrary to conventional wisdom, in the corporate world the real thief of time is not procrastination. It is interruptions!

Several studies have been conducted to quantify exactly how much time is lost on average for each interruption. The findings range from 64 seconds to 23 minutes and 15 seconds per interruption to get back to where you were, mentally, immediately before the interruption.

Other studies have looked at how many times per day the average office worker is interrupted. One of the most widely accepted studies indicates that it is every 10.5 minutes. That is 1 000 times per month! So, if each interruption wastes a minimu of a minute, at least 1 000 minutes per person are wasted every month in your average organisation. Think about that.

Unless and until the corporate culture places a specific focus on the use of time and its wastage, this is the unfortunate reality.

• The myth of business efficiencies

Many businesses portray business efficiencies as some sort of mythical creature, and the focus is inevitably placed on refining, redoing and replacing policies and procedures. But efficiency is focused on reducing the wastage of resources in whatever you do, including, and in particular, the invaluable resource – time!

So, regardless of the policies, processes and procedures that are or are not in place, business efficiency is a matter of common sense and, crucially, the prevailing culture. Urgency, interruptions and general abuse and wastage of time happen – in many cases routinely – not *because* of the policies, processes and procedures that exist, but *in spite* of them.

If the corporate culture does not actively recognise and respect the value of every person's time, inefficiencies will prevail – regardless of policies, processes and procedures.

- ## Work smart, not hard!

"Working smart", as I understand it, is simply finding ways of completing the same tasks using less effort and energy. The concept of working smart, therefore, cannot coexist with a culture that glorifies those who work long hours and frowns upon those who leave on time. Or with a culture where people are not trusted with flexitime and other similar tools aimed at improving efficiencies.

- ## Business processes

Many businesses have numerous and lengthy business processes that are filed away somewhere, with most of the people within the organisation not knowing what these processes say. They have been crafted, in many cases, so that they are seen to exist when auditors and regulators come around. If this is the motivation behind these processes, then it is a losing battle from the onset.

The way people go about their daily duties, in many cases, pays little regard to the processes that are seen, by external parties, to exist. For all intents and purposes, to the people within the company, going about their daily duties, these business processes do not actually exist.

Effective business processes require an appreciation and understanding of all the required inputs, across all sections and departments, and of how they all tie in with each other. Without this understanding and appreciation, documented business processes will never be more that theoretical. They will always be seen to exist from the outside rather than actually existing within the organisation.

• When managers don't manage

Management and being a manager require a certain skillset which is quite different and distinct from the technical skillset one may have. This is something that is surprisingly often overlooked or not even realised in the corporate world. The result is that a certain culture has developed in many organisations – a culture where people are rewarded for technical competence and long service by being promoted to the position of manager. Yet these people don't know how to manage and, therefore, *they do not* manage!

Another common aspect of the corporate culture in many organisations is the refusal of senior managers to let go of the reins and allow middle and lower managers to actually manage – which includes making decisions. As a result, middle and lower managers are reduced to doers of ad hoc tasks.

If the culture does not place a deliberate emphasis on ensuring that people actually know what it is to manage, yet they are allowed to effectively manage, managers will continue to *not* manage.

• "We value our people."

We've all heard this from corporates. Probably far too often. Yet the situation on the ground more often than not says something quite different.

Employees are people. Being an employee is only one aspect of any person's life. And, most interestingly, almost every person only gets up and goes to work, fulfilling this role as an employee, in order to make the other aspects of their life better. When people are routinely overexerted and drained – mentally and physically – in their capacity as employees to the extent that the other aspects of life are compromised, there is a problem. A serious problem!

If employees are genuinely valued, there will be a constant and deliberate acknowledgement and appreciation, first and foremost, that these are people and not machines or "just another resource" that the business makes use of; and, second, that being an employee of this organisation is merely one of the many aspects of every person's life. They have lives outside the workplace.

• "How are you adding value?"

And then, against this backdrop that "we value our people", comes the frequently asked question, "How are you adding value?"

This is less of a question and more of a thinly veiled attack. It is a statement that the person facing this "question" is, in fact, *not* adding value. And, regardless of what answer is given, the conclusion has probably already been drawn. The correct answer would be, "I am adding value by competently filling a role deemed necessary by this organisation." If there are issues around competence or job description, those would be and should be the real questions, and dealing with these issues is part of good management and leadership.

"How are you adding value?" on the other hand, is a question pregnant with toxicity, and it betrays an equally toxic culture of bad management and bad leadership. It is a corporate culture where there is inherent derision rather than value for people.

• Teamwork or picking up someone's slack?

Another overused term in many organisations. And another term that, while ostensibly positive, is pregnant with negative undertones. It is often used as a way to justify the manipulation of colleagues into tidying up your mess.

But many organisations have an *Animal Farm* culture, where some animals are simply more equal than others. This means that the more equal animals in more equal departments routinely dump their incomplete work on the desks of the less equal animals in less equal departments to tidy up before moving forward. And it is done, ostensibly, in the name of teamwork.

Teamwork, in its positive sense, entails each person doing their part fully and properly and, only then, handing it over to the next person to take the process forward. But this doesn't work if the culture doesn't support it.

• Employee engagement

Employee engagement is a measure of the extent to which the employees believe that the employer is discharging its unwritten, moral obligations. Its obligations that do not form part of the written employment contract. And quite simply, engaged employees are more productive and more valuable. Engaged employees will go beyond expectation because they want to, and not because of fear.

In extreme cases, disengaged employees will actively sabotage the business!

Together with cultural entropy, this constitutes the best way of measuring the corporate culture. And let's remember the words of Professor Robert Kaplan: "If you can't measure it, you can't manage it, and if you can't manage it, you can't change it."

• Final word

Business strategies fail, and business targets are not met, not for the common reasons that are bandied about, including bad business strategies, bad business plans, bad processes and procedures, and incompetent staff. It is because of a bad culture. In many cases, a toxic culture!

You can have the best strategies, the best plans,

and the best processes and procedures, but if the underlying corporate culture is one that does not support any or all of those, they may as well not exist!

Culture is king!

By purchasing this book – *Corporate Culture Demystified* (paperback or ebook) – you qualify to receive a FREE PDF version of *Life Demystified* IMMEDIATELY, as well as selected free chapters of forthcoming publications on an ongoing basis.

Simply email: lifedemystified.inc@gmail.com.

OTHER TITLES IN THE DEMYSTIFIED SERIES

(Current and forthcoming)

- *Life Demystified: Understanding – The Secret to Success*
- *Goal-Setting Demystified* (forthcoming)
- *Corporate Law Demystified: The Essential Legal Handbook for Business Leaders* (forthcoming)
- *The Corporate Conspiracy Demystified: Brainwash and Bullsh!t* (forthcoming)
- *Weight-Loss Demystified* (forthcoming)

For updates on forthcoming titles and events, you can follow Marc on various platforms:

Amazon Author Page
https://www.amazon.com/author/marcpillay

https://www.facebook.com/marcpillay.demystifyinglife/

@MarcPillay3

@pillay_marc

REFERENCES

1. See https://www.facebook.com/EpicCultureCo/posts/every-ceo-is-in-fact-a-chief-cultural-officer-the-terrifying-thing-is-its-the-ce/2445522899026090/ (accessed 2 April 2020).

2. Pillay, M. (2019), *Life Demystified: Understanding – The Secret to Success*, Second Edition, pp. 94–98.

3. "What is Cultural Entropy", SMARTMINDS, https://smartminds.io/cultural-entropy-fear-driven-energy/ (accessed 2 April 2020).

4. Horubet, L. (3 March 2018), "Cultural Entropy and Cultural Risk", Let's Talk Leadership Consultancy, https://lets-talk-more.com/cultural-entropy/ (accessed 2 April 2020).

5. "Cultural Entropy – The Untapped Potential in Your Company", Culture Leadership Group, http://95percent.co/wp-content/uploads/2017/03/Joanna-Barclay-Cultural-Entropy-The-Untapped-Potential-In-Your-Organization-27th-February-2017.pdf (accessed 2 April 2020).

6. "Glossary: Cultural Entropy", Old Mutual Limited, https://www.oldmutual.com/investor-relations/glossary/cultural-entropy (accessed 2 April 2020).

7. Pillay, M. *Life Demystified*.

8. Francke, A. (2014), *Financial Times Guide to Management: How to Make a Difference and Get Results* (Upper Saddle River: FT Press), p. 115.

9. Vermeulen, F. (8 November 2017), "Many Strategies Fail Because They're Not Actually Strategies", *Harvard Business Review*, https://hbr.org/2017/11/many-strategies-fail-because-theyre-not-actually-strategies (accessed 2 April 2020).

10. Clason, G.S. (1926), *The Richest Man in Babylon*, p. ix.

11. Pillay, M. *Life Demystified*, pp. 85–93.

12. Tracy, B. (2017), *Eat that Frog: Get More of the Important Things Done Today* (London: Hodder & Stoughton), p. 21.

13. Schulte, B. (1 June 2015), "Work Interruptions Can Cost You 6 Hours a Day: An Efficiency Expert Explains How to Avoid Them", *The Washington Post*, https://www.washingtonpost.com/news/inspired-life/wp/2015/06/01/interruptions-at-work-can-cost-you-up-to-6-hours-a-day-heres-how-to-avoid-them/ (accessed 2 April 2020).

14. Tracy, B. *Eat that Frog*, pp. 12–14.

15. Pattison, K. (28 July 2008), "Worker, Interrupted: The Cost of Task Switching", *Fast Company*, https://www.fastcompany.com/944128/worker-interrupted-cost-task-switching (accessed 2 April 2020).

16. Dawson, R., Jackson, T. and Wilson, D. (2001), "The Cost of Email Interruption", *Journal of Systems and Information Technology* 5(1), pp. 81–92, https://repository.lboro.ac.uk/articles/The_cost_of_email_interruption_/9402233 (accessed 2 April 2020).

17. Pillay, M. *Life Demystified*.

18. Orwell, G. (1945), *Animal Farm: A Fairy Story*.

19. Pillay, M. *Life Demystified*, pp. 55–77.

www.ingramcontent.com/pod-product-compliance
Lightning Source LLC
Chambersburg PA
CBHW030519210326
41597CB00013B/965